Some years ago, the distinguished theologian Jean-Marc Berthoud reintroduced twenty-first-century readers to a long-neglected giant of the Reformation: Pierre Viret (1511–1571). Viret was not only a close companion of John Calvin but also a theologian and thinker of exceptional stature. His vast body of work — remarkable both in scope and depth, spanning apologetics, biblical law, ethics, economics, and political philosophy — stands alongside that of the great Reformer of Geneva. Since that recovery, we have witnessed a steady republication and translation of Viret's writings, bringing the legacy of this extraordinary man and exemplary minister back into the light.

In a similar spirit, Cántaro Publications, under the leadership of Steven R. Martins, has dedicated itself to recovering and sharing the riches of the Reformed tradition. Since our first correspondence, Steven has become a valued partner in the work of disseminating sound theological resources in Portuguese through a publishing house based in Brazil of which I have the privilege to direct. Particularly noteworthy is the series *The Old Spanish Reformers*, which introduces the writings of many lesser-known Reformers—not only to my homeland of Brazil but to a much broader audience eager to rediscover these treasures.

This volume, *Dialogue of Christian Doctrine* by Juan de Valdés (1490–1541), is a precious addition to that collection. Though unfamiliar to many today, Valdés counted among his associates prominent figures such as Peter Martyr Vermigli and Giulia Gonzaga. His *Dialogue of Christian Doctrine* is a catechetical exposition of Christian doctrine, presented entirely in the form of a dialogue—a literary form often and skillfully employed by Pierre Viret himself. The result is a text that is both accessible and enriching, offering much to neophytes as well as to those already deeply rooted in sound doctrine.

May God be pleased to use this and other works to further the spread of the Gospel and the advance of Christ's Kingdom across the earth, among Hispanic peoples and beyond.

*Te alaben los pueblos, oh Dios;*
*Todos los pueblos te alaben* (Salmo 67:3).

**FELIPE SABINO**, Founder & Editorial Director of Editora Monergismo, Brazil

*The Old Spanish Reformers* series, published by the Cántaro Institute under the direction of Rev. Steven R. Martins, is a remarkable undertaking that will ultimately comprise thirty-one volumes, bringing the spiritual riches of the Spanish Reformation to English-speaking readers. The latest volume, *Dialogue of Christian Doctrine*, was first published anonymously in 1529 in Alcalá de Henares. Its author, Juan de Valdés, was denounced to the Inquisition for heresy as a result of this work, but, after receiving a timely warning, fled to Italy—where, curiously, his teachings were met with papal approval. Framed as a conversation between Eusebius, a priest named Antonio, and an archbishop, Valdés' doctrine is marked by such clarity and evangelical purity that it continues to resonate with sincere Christians, both Roman Catholic and Protestant alike.

> DR. ADOLFO GARCÍA DE LA SIENRA (Ph.D.), Research Professor
> of the Institute of Philosophy at the Universidad Veracruzana, Mexico

We rarely glimpse the Reformation at work in individual hearts. Yet this remarkable dialogue—written at the height of the Spanish Inquisition—draws us into that very process in sixteenth-century Spain. In an age when reformist voices were silenced, the first rays of gospel renewal broke through. Here we see God at work, captivating minds and stirring souls to depend wholly on His grace, His Word, and the power of His Spirit. More than a historical artifact, this work stands as a living testimony to the gospel's power to awaken, instruct, and transform—a must-read for all who long to witness how God was preparing hearts to embrace the Reformation.

> REV. JOSÉ PORTILLO, Executive Director of Hispanic Leadership
> Initiative (HLI), Planter and Pastor of Vive Charlotte Church, PCA, USA

In an age marked by spiritual confusion and historical amnesia, *The Old Spanish Reformers: Dialogue of Christian Doctrine* provides a timely and edifying recovery of a forgotten Reformation voice. Juan de Valdés' theological clarity and pastoral warmth shine through in this masterful translation, which preserves the original's devotional depth while making it accessible to today's readers. As a pastor serving in a Hispanic church-planting context, I find this work not only historically significant but also profoundly relevant for the church today. Steven R. Martins and the editorial team have given the global church a rare gift—one that calls for careful reading, reflection, and faithful application.

> REV. JOSE DANIEL FASOLINO, Lead Pastor of Emmanuel Baptist
> Church East, EBCE, Ajax, Ontario, Canada

VOLUME 31

# THE OLD
# SPANISH
# REFORMERS

## DIALOGUE OF
## CHRISTIAN DOCTRINE

VOLUME 31

# THE OLD SPANISH REFORMERS

## DIALOGUE OF CHRISTIAN DOCTRINE

JUAN DE VALDÉS

GENERAL EDITOR
Steven R. Martins

cántaro
publications

cántaro
publications

cantaroinstitute.org

*The Old Spanish Reformers, Vol. 31: Dialogue of Christian Doctrine*
Translated by Steven R. Martins, from the 1922 edition,
aided by consulting the 1979 edition (Madrid: Editora Nacional).
Published by Cántaro Publications, a publishing imprint of the Cántaro Institute,
Jordan Station, Ontario, Canada

Series General Editor: Steven R. Martins
Translator: Steven R. Martins
Book Design by Cántaro Institute

For volume pricing, please contact
info@cantaroinstitute.org

Library & Archives Canada
ISBN: 978-1-998711-12-3

Printed in the United States of America

This labour of love is dedicated to
**Nehemías Agustín Martins,**
my beloved son.

—Steven

# The Old Spanish Reformers

# Table of Contents

# Series Preface

IN THE YEAR 1847, the Spanish scholar and Hebraist Luis de Usoz y Río (1805-1865) published what would be the first volume of *The Old Spanish Reformers* (*Los Reformistas Antiguos Españoles*), a work that would consist of twenty-four volumes altogether, with its final volume published posthumously in 1880. This compilation of writings of the sixteenth-century Spanish reformers, updated by Usoz y Río to nineteenth century Castilian, had not been made widely available to modern-day readership. Nor had it been translated in its entirety to the English language. The most recent print edition was a limited facsimile reproduction in 1983, of which the Cántaro Institute was able to acquire a complete set from an antiquarian bookstore in Madrid, Spain. In light of its lack of accessibility, and as part of the Cántaro Institute's mission to recover the literary treasures of the protestant reformation, the Institute hereby presents the first English translation of *The Old Spanish Reformers*.

### Editorial Notes

To the keen observer it will become apparent that some texts have not been translated, particularly those originally written in Latin. This was a decision made in light of the importance of preserving the historic character of the original volumes. Furthermore, Scriptural references have been translated from the Spanish text cited by the respective writers, instead of utilizing modern English translation versions. This allows us to preserve the Spanish character of the original writings. Exceptions to this will be noted with the abbreviation mark of contemporary Bible translation versions (e.g., ESV, NKJV, etc.).

On the matter of publishing for the first time this series of *The Old Spanish Reformers* in English, the reader will also come to realize that there are more than twenty-four volumes in this current print edition. The reason for the *expansion* of this set was to include those works by the Spanish reformers which were not compiled by Usoz y Río. Whether the documents were not available to him at the time (such as those of Dr. Constantino Ponce de la Fuente, Casiodoro de Reina, Antonio del Corro, etc.) or if he was not able to complete the collection in time is not something we can know with any certainty. However, an expansion of this set with other works by the Spanish Reformers can be seen as a fitting tribute to Usoz y Río and his herculean effort to preserve what are otherwise forgotten works from the sixteenth century Protestant reformation.

A clarifying anecdote in relation to this volume of *The Old Spanish Reformers: Dialogue of Christian Doctrine* by Juan de Valdés is notable for containing both Protestant and Roman Catholic elements. This duality raises questions, especially considering that Valdés would later become a key figure in the Spanish Reformation. The explanation lies in the approximate date of its composition—before Valdés fully broke from the Roman Catholic Church. He was only eighteen at the time, and the work was significantly influenced by one of his professors, who reviewed and advised revisions to the original manuscript. As a result, the final version does not fully reflect Valdés' Reformed convictions. Where the text appears to deviate from Protestant doctrine, it is reasonable to attribute such statements not to Valdés himself, but to the intervention of his Catholic mentor, who likely shaped the work to ensure its acceptance by Roman Catholic readers and its safety from Inquisitorial censure. Nevertheless, the overall tone of the *Dialogue* is unmistakably Protestant, and it holds historical significance as the first popular Protestant catechism—preceding both Martin Luther's Small and Large Catechisms, which appeared later that same year (1529).

## The Publisher's Intent

It is the earnest hope of the Cántaro Institute that this present print edition of *The Old Spanish Reformers* not only furnishes the church with an invaluable literary, Protestant treasure but also sparks within it a reformational spirit and fans it to flame. The reformers sought to bring glory to God in all life and thought, we should imitate them and seek to do the same, guided by the inscripturated revelation of God which is illuminated by His Holy Spirit.

## Acknowledgments

The Cántaro Institute would like to thank the Hultink Family Foundation (HFF), the Hispanic Leadership Initiative (HLI), and Sevilla Chapel for their generous financial support which brought to realization this modern print edition of *The Old Spanish Reformers*. The Institute would also like to thank all those who type-copied the original works, those who assisted with translation and editing, and those who advised and aided us in our research. This invaluable protestant treasure has been recovered and restored for the good of the church and for the glory of God. And with one voice we can say: "For us there is one God, the Father, from whom are all things and for whom we exist, and one Lord, Jesus Christ, through whom are all things and through whom we exist" (1 Cor. 8:6).

*Soli Deo Gloria*

# *The Dialogue of Doctrine (1529)*

Juan de Valdés

To the most illustrious Lord Don Diego López Pacheco,
Marquis of Villena, Duke of Escalona,
Count of San Esteban, etc.

**The Author**

# Introduction[1]

O NE DAY, most illustrious Lord, while passing through a town in these Kingdoms, and upon learning that, by the order of the Lord of that town, and even at his own expense, the priests were teaching the children the principles and rudiments of Christian Doctrine in their churches—a practice I had long desired to see implemented—I decided to join the children in one of the churches. My intention was not only to learn something beneficial that I could introduce into my monastery but also to observe whether there might be any aspect of this noble and heavenly endeavor where I, with my knowledge and experience, could offer assistance and enhance the work.

Although the priest who was teaching was uneducated and not as well-grounded in the matters he spoke of as would be

1. Originally titled *Diálogo de Doctrina Cristiana* and published anonymously in 1529 in Alcalá de Henares, this work by Juan de Valdés (c.1509–1541) was written with a didactic purpose: to instruct young readers—particularly children and the unlearned—in the essentials of the Christian faith. In a conversational style, Valdés unfolds the Apostles' Creed, the Ten Commandments, and the Lord's Prayer—three foundational elements of Christian teaching which, strikingly, he treats in the very same order later adopted by the Heidelberg Catechism some three decades afterward, as observed by Dr. Theodore Van Raalte of the Canadian Reformed Theological Seminary (CRTS). Juan was the twin brother of Alfonso de Valdés, a humanist and imperial secretary to Charles V, and while Alfonso remained within the circles of Catholic reform, Juan's theological journey led him toward a more evangelical understanding of Scripture and salvation. A brief biographical profile of Valdés is provided at the end of this publication.

necessary, given the importance of the subject, I found solace and took pleasure in spending a considerable amount of time there. When the priest had finished, and noticing me among his students, wearing my religious habit, he approached me. He expressed, as he said, a desire to know my thoughts on what I had heard him say. Seeing his good intentions and judging that, though uneducated, he was capable and teachable, and recognizing the benefit that could come from advising him, I praised, as was fitting, his good and holy work, encouraging him to continue and to exhort and advise others to do the same.

Furthermore, I suggested that we both go together to discuss this matter with Don Fray Pedro de Alba, Archbishop of Granada. Besides the importance of ensuring that such a truly Christian and evangelical initiative be carried out under his authority as a prelate, I believed that he, as a person of sacred learning and Christian spirit, could provide us with extensive instruction. This way, not only would we both be edified in what concerned us, but we would also be instructed in those things necessary for teaching others.

The priest found my counsel very agreeable; therefore, without further delay, he left his house and church, and I set aside the journey I was on (for the greater reason should always take precedence over the lesser). Together, we went in search of the Lord Archbishop, whom, by divine providence (as God often aids and favors good intentions), we found at a Monastery of his Order, where he had retreated for a few days to escape the burdensome affairs that accompany his position. His Lordship received us with great kindness and charity, not only because this was his custom, but also because I was somewhat known to him, which further enhanced his cordiality.

When he learned the reason for our visit, after we had risen from dining with him at his table, he took us by the hands, saying that he wished to spend the entire afternoon with us. He led us to a garden within the Monastery; and as we sat by a fountain—since this was around the time of the Feast of St. John—we openly presented our case. His Lordship responded at great length, fully satisfying not only the priest, who was somewhat distant from understanding what was necessary for the children he instructed, but also me, who believed I had a moderate grasp of the subject.

Given your Lordship's pleasure in such matters, never tiring of reading or discussing them, I wished that you might know what transpired there, as well as all those who share the same interest and affection as your Lordship. Thus, I decided to write it all down as it came to mind in this brief account. And because it would be tedious and tiresome to repeatedly write "the Archbishop said," "the priest said," and "I said," I resolved to present it in such a way that each person speaks for himself, making it more of a dialogue than a treatise. This way, when the reader hears the Archbishop speak, they may pay close attention to the grave, pious, and learned words of that excellent man, for your Lordship may consider it as if you are hearing him and not me.

# Eusebius the monk, Antronio the Priest, and the Archbishop of Granada

**A**RCHBISHOP: Your holy zeal, my dear brothers, with which you desire to know these matters you have raised, is so commendable that I cannot help but praise you for it. I also greatly value the effort you have undertaken in seeking me out as a teacher and guide for your good intentions. Although I may not have the sufficient knowledge and experience that would be ideal to satisfy your inquiries, I place great hope in the supreme goodness and magnificence of God. I trust that, seeing your eagerness to learn and my sincere willingness to fulfill your requests, He will grant wisdom and understanding to my heart and open my mouth to provide the answers that will satisfy both myself and you.

This is what He has done in the past with many prophets and individuals of lowly and humble understanding. Moreover, since our Lord Jesus Christ promised that He would be present in our conversations whenever two or three of us are gathered in His name, we can believe that He is present with us here as we have gathered in His name. He will illuminate our hearts with His Spirit so that what we discuss here may be for the glory of His most holy name and for the edification not only of our souls but also of those who have entrusted theirs to our care.

Let us proceed in this manner: to better accommodate your preferences, you shall ask me all that you wish to know, and I will respond according to the wisdom and understanding that God grants me.

**Eusebius:** Your Lordship has spoken both matters in a most Christian and excellent manner.

**Archbishop:** There's no need for such formalities now; since we are here alone, I don't want you to address me with any more courtesy than I would extend to you.

**Eusebius:** I am just as pleased with what you say now as with what you said earlier. Since that's the case, I will let the priest ask his questions first, and if any doubts remain, I will follow up with my own questions.

**Antronio:** It would be much better if you were the one to ask, as you are more capable of framing the questions according to what you wish to know, and you have shared your thoughts with me. In this way, I will feel more satisfied and better instructed.

**Eusebius:** As you command. I am happy to do as you wish. Since I am to begin, I would like to start the discussion from the very beginning of Christianity, so that with God's grace, we may bring it to completion. So, tell us first, why are we called by this name, "Christian," and where did it originate?

**Archbishop:** We are called Christians because, just as those who were of the lineage of Israel were called Israelites, so it is fitting that we, who have faith in Jesus Christ, should be called Christians. The first place where this name was used was in Antioch. The reason was that the Apostles, seeing the growing number of those who embraced their preaching, thought it proper that all who confessed faith in Jesus Christ and observed Christ's evangelical law should be called Christians.

**Eusebius:** What is the difference between a Christian and a non-Christian?

**Archbishop:** The Christian, after receiving the water of baptism, is primarily founded in faith and charity, then in benefiting all and harming none, and ultimately in living purely and sincerely according to the example of Jesus Christ, Our Lord.

**Eusebius:** And if we were to see someone who embodies all these qualities, should we consider them a Christian?

**Archbishop:** Yes, why not?

**Eusebius:** Because we might be greatly deceived.

**Archbishop:** How so?

**Eusebius:** I will explain. As for faith and charity, which are inner virtues, you see that we cannot judge whether someone possesses them or not. The other qualities can also be found in a non-believer, as we read of many pagans who possessed them.

**Archbishop:** I understand your point; you mean to say that, in addition to what I mentioned, it is also necessary for a Christian to observe the ceremonies and statutes of the Church.

**Eusebius:** You understood me perfectly.

**Archbishop:** Consider, Father, that what I stated a Christian must possess is the essence; the other matters are merely ancillary. Just as we do not consider someone a Christian if they do not observe the Church's ceremonies, I would assert that we should likewise not consider someone a Christian if they do not fulfill the primary obligations I mentioned earlier. However, the judgments of the common people, and even those above the common people, are so corrupted in this regard that when I reflect on it, I am deeply pained. But we may discuss this further on another occasion.

**Eusebius:** Indeed, you have answered far better than one of our lay brothers, whom I once asked in jest what he thought was the difference between Christians and Moors. He replied that he knew of no other difference than that we do not eat meat during Lent while they do, and that we observe Sundays and feast days while they do not. If it pleases you, the young man who gave this answer had been a lay brother for thirty years.

**Archbishop:** Clearly, he had learned very little from your company. It seems he was more devoted to bacon than to books. But, returning to our topic, it is essential that a Christian bears the mark of Christianity that Our Lord Jesus Christ gave to the Apostles when He said: "By this, everyone will know that you are my disciples if you love one another." Just as we do not consider someone a friar of St. Jerome if they do not wear the distinctive habit, since some say, "This is the sign that St. Jerome left to his friars," it is equally reasonable that we do not consider someone a Christian if they do not bear the sign that Jesus Christ left to His followers.

**Eusebius:** That is very well stated. And since we are to discuss how a Christian should be instructed in the doctrine of Jesus Christ, tell us, what is the first thing that should be taught to a Christian?

**Archbishop:** As you know from what is entrusted to the god-parents of children at baptism, the most important thing is to instruct them in the faith and in good and holy customs, and to teach them the *Pater Noster*, the *Ave Maria*,[2] and the *Credo*. You must emphasize this with great earnestness and sincerity, and you should also instruct their parents to do the same—not just when the child is baptized, but whenever the opportunity arises. Additionally, they should be urged to take great care and vigilance so that their children's minds are not corrupted by bad company or harmful conversations. As far as possible, they should keep their children away from anything unchristian and encourage them to love and adhere to the doctrine of Jesus Christ, so much so that they take delight and pleasure even in mentioning His name. Furthermore, you should advise them to be very careful about whom they entrust with their children's education, ensuring that they are taught both good morals and literacy. Encourage them to find a teacher who is both a virtuous man and of good and holy customs, so that the

---

2.   **Editor's Note:** The inclusion of the *Ave Maria* marks the point at which the influence of Valdés' Roman Catholic editor becomes evident; the work was originally a distinctly Protestant composition.

children learn both knowledge and holiness from him.

**Antronio:** And what should be done by those who cannot afford to do this?

**Archbishop:** Advise everyone to follow this counsel, and those who lack the means to do so should at least do what they can. Believe me, if the wealthy and influential took heed of this advice, they would not do what we all too often see them doing, to the great detriment of Christendom.

**Antronio:** What is it that they do?

**Archbishop:** I will tell you. It seems that they are more concerned with making a good mule out of a young horse than with making good Christians out of their children.

**Antronio:** In what way?

**Archbishop:** In this way: We see that when it comes to the mule, they only entrust it to someone who knows how to handle it very well, ensuring that it walks properly and doesn't trot, and that it is well trained and not spoiled. But when it comes to their children, they don't bother to check whether the tutor or teacher they hire is a person of good morals or bad, free from vices or vicious, a friend of virtues and goodness or inclined towards wickedness and corruption, and ultimately, whether he is a good Christian or not. Instead, they only care about superficial things: whether he has a good appearance, as they say, to present himself well among nobles, and whether he is of noble lineage. These are qualities from which the poor child may gain little benefit, but instead, he often incurs significant harm. And just as such children absorb worldly habits at a tender age, it is difficult for them to rid themselves of these habits later on. As this behavior is observed among the elite, whom everyone considers role models, you can be sure that many others will follow suit. So, you see, if this were corrected, what great benefit it would bring to Christendom!

**Antronio:** By my faith, you are absolutely right, and I am extremely pleased with what you are saying. I promise you that I will follow this advice from now on. But tell me, what do you think I should first and foremost teach the children who regularly attend my church?

**Archbishop:** I will tell you this in the same order that I have resolved it should be done throughout my entire archdiocese. Thus, I say that the first thing to do is to frequently remind them of the vow they made at baptism and to make sure they clearly understand it.

**Antronio:** What is this vow you mention? I neither know of it nor have I ever heard of such a vow.

**Archbishop:** How can that be? When you baptize a child, don't the godparents promise on their behalf that the child will live and die in the faith and doctrine of Jesus Christ? And as a sign of this, don't you have them recite the *Credo*?

**Antronio:** Yes, I do.

**Archbishop:** Then, doesn't it seem to you that this is making a vow?

**Antronio:** Upon my word, you speak the truth! I had never considered it in that way, even though I believe I have baptized more than five hundred boys and girls in this world. I had never thought there were other vows besides those taken by monks.

**Eusebius:** That is well. You can explain that to us later; for now, please tell us what should be taught after that.

**Archbishop:** After the *Credo*, the Ten Commandments should be taught. It is essential that they know how to please the One in whom they already believe and how to fulfill His will, which is entirely contained within the Commandments. You should explain them thoroughly and make it clear that to be true Christians, they must not break even the smallest of these Commandments. Along with these Commandments, it would be beneficial to teach them the fifth, sixth, and seventh chapters of the Gospel of Matthew, as these contain the essence and fulfillment of Christian Doctrine. In teaching them this, strive to make them cherish and love the evangelical doctrine, helping them understand that it is a light yoke and an easy burden for those who embrace it with love and devotion.

Then, you should instruct them on what to avoid, to live with continual caution. Here, you should discuss the seven deadly sins, explaining them in such a way that they begin to detest them from a young age. It is also important that they learn about the gifts of the Holy Spirit, the theological virtues, and other similar teachings. Additionally, you should give a very holy and brief explanation of the *Pater Noster*, emphasizing its significance so that they value it as they should, and do not pray it mindlessly like many of the ignorant do, not knowing what they are saying.

**Antronio:** And do you think it would be good to also accustom them to some devout prayers alongside this?

**Archbishop:** In that matter, you may do as you see fit. Here, I am only addressing what every Christian must know; I won't venture into other matters. Beyond this, it would be very beneficial to teach them, in a concise and systematic way, the whole narrative of Sacred Scripture, summarizing everything from the creation of the heavens and the earth and all that is in them, up to the most glorious coming of our Lord and God, Jesus Christ.

**Antronio:** I would like you to explain that to me, as you must know it well.

**Archbishop:** Indeed, I do know it, and I will explain it to you, but at the appropriate time.

**Eusebius:** You speak wisely, and since you mentioned that the first thing children should be taught is the *Credo*, it is necessary that you tell us what should be said to them about each article of it.

**Archbishop:** I am willing. Ask me about it in the manner you wish to understand, and I will respond. In this way, it will be explained such that the priest can take from it what he thinks is most suitable for his students.

**Antronio:** Let it be so.

**Eusebius:** The first article states: *I believe in God, the Father Almighty, Creator of heaven and earth.*

**Archbishop:** That is indeed the truth.

**Eusebius:** Now, let us consider: when we say "God," what should we understand by it?

**Archbishop:** We should understand that God is an eternal being who never had a beginning and will never have an end, and that there is nothing in existence that can equal Him in greatness or wisdom. He, with His will alone, created all things, both visible and invisible, and with His marvelous wisdom, He governs and directs all things. With His supreme goodness, He nourishes and preserves all things; and He also redeemed the human race from the misery into which it had fallen through the sin of the first man.

**Eusebius:** Let's consider, then: what benefit can be derived from contemplating these three aspects of God?

**Archbishop:** I will tell you: When we contemplate His omnipotence, we fully submit ourselves to Him, recognizing that before His majesty, the grandeur of both men and angels is nothing. Thus, with great faith and complete certainty, we believe all the things recorded in Sacred Scripture that He has done; and we also believe that what He has promised will indeed come to pass. From this, we come to distrust our own strength, which is truly weak and frail, and we wholeheartedly place ourselves in the hands of the One who can do all that He wills. When we reflect on His supreme wisdom, we disregard our own wisdom and that of any other human being, but we believe that everything He does, He does rightly and justly, even if some things may seem absurd to human judgment. When we consider His supreme goodness, we clearly see that there is nothing in us that we do not owe to His magnificent generosity. We also understand that there is no sin, however grave, that He is not willing to forgive if the sinner truly turns back to Him in repentance. Moreover, we believe that there is nothing in the world that He is not willing to grant to those who ask with complete trust.

**Eusebius:** And now, let us consider: do you believe that it is sufficient to merely believe that God is as you have described?

**Archbishop:** No, not at all; on the contrary, it is necessary that, in addition to this, we place all our love, hope, and trust in Him with a sincere and pure heart. We must abhor and curse Satan, along with all idolatry and every form of magical arts, and worship God alone. There should be nothing that we hold in higher regard or esteem than Him—neither angels, nor parents, nor rulers, nor wealth, nor honors, nor pleasures. We must be prepared to sacrifice our lives for His cause, with the complete and firm assurance that the one who entrusts everything to Him cannot perish.

**Eusebius:** Let us consider: is there anything else we ought to honor, fear, or love, apart from the one true God?

**Archbishop:** If we honor anything, fear anything, or love anything outside of Him, we must do so for His sake, attributing everything to His glory, and always giving thanks to Him for whatever may happen to us, whether it be sorrowful or joyful.

**Antronio:** Tell us, my lord, is this requirement for everyone?

**Archbishop:** Yes, without a doubt; it applies to all who wish to partake in the passion of Jesus Christ, and not just to some more than others.

**Eusebius:** Very well, let us continue.

The second article is to *believe in Jesus Christ, the Son of God, our one Lord and God.*

**Archbishop:** That is correct.

**Eusebius:** So tell us, how could it be that Jesus Christ was both immortal God and mortal man?

**Archbishop:** This was an easy thing to accomplish for Him who can do all that He wills. Moreover, besides believing that Jesus Christ is such because of the divine nature He shares with the Father, we must attribute to the Son everything we attribute to the Father in terms of greatness, wisdom, and goodness. We must also believe that everything we owe to the Father, we equally owe to the Son. It is true that the eternal Father willed to create all things and give them to us through the Son.

**Eusebius:** Why does Sacred Scripture refer to the Son as "Son"?

**Archbishop:** Because it is proper to the Son to be begotten and to be born of the eternal Father.

**Eusebius:** Why does it call Him the "only" Son?

**Archbishop:** To distinguish between the natural Son, who is Jesus Christ, and the adoptive sons, who are all those who are drawn near and united with Him through the bond of love.

**Eusebius:** Let us consider, then, why did God will that His Son, being God, should become a man?

**Archbishop:** So that through a man, humanity might be reconciled with God.

**Antronio:** I am exceedingly pleased to hear you speak, for although one asks good questions, the other answers even better.

**Eusebius:** I assure you, you will hear things that will amaze you even more.

The third article is to *believe that Jesus Christ was conceived by the work of the Holy Spirit and that He was born of the Virgin Mary.* Tell us why He willed to be born in this manner.

**Archbishop:** It was fitting for God to be born in this way, and it was necessary for the One who came to cleanse the impurities and defilements of our birth to be born in this manner. God willed to be born as a human child so that we, being reborn through His power in a new spiritual birth, might be born as children of God.

**Eusebius:** And tell me, should we believe that this same Jesus Christ lived here in the world, performed those miracles, and taught those things that the Evangelists recount?

**Archbishop:** We should believe this even more firmly than we believe that I am a man.

**Eusebius:** Then, should we also believe that this is the Messiah who was foreshadowed in the figures of the old law, whom the prophets promised, and whom the Jews had long awaited?

**Archbishop:** Yes, without any doubt, and in the same way, you must believe that to attain complete and perfect holiness, it is sufficient to imitate and follow the life and teachings of Jesus Christ Himself.

**Eusebius:** I am well satisfied with these past three articles.

The fourth article, as you know, is to *believe that this same Jesus Christ, our Lord, suffered death and passion during the time of Pontius Pilate, and that He was crucified, died, and was buried.*

**Archbishop:** Indeed, I know; but it is also important to understand that He was the spotless Lamb and that He suffered all these things willingly, without any fault of His own, and as one who greatly desired to suffer for our salvation. Moreover, it was all according to the will of His Eternal Father.

**Eusebius:** Tell us more, why did the Father will that His dearly beloved Son, who was innocence itself, should suffer such cruel, unworthy, and terrible things?

**Archbishop:** So that through this most exalted sacrifice, we might be reconciled with Him when we place all our trust and hope for our justification in His name.

**Eusebius:** Tell us another thing, why did God allow the entire human race to fall in such a way? And, having allowed it, couldn't He have restored us by another means?

**Archbishop:** This understanding does not come from human reason, which comprehends very little of such matters, but from faith. Faith tells me that there was no better or more beneficial way to accomplish our restoration.

**Antronio:** There is something I have long wished to know, which I would like to ask you: why did Jesus Christ choose to die by this particular manner of death rather than another?

**Archbishop:** Because it was prophesied in this way, and because the world regarded this manner of death as the most dishonorable of all, due to its cruel and severe torments. Therefore, it was fitting that He who, with arms extended toward all parts of the world, invites all peoples to salvation and eternal life, should die such a death. Moreover, it was to call those who are immersed in worldly cares to enjoy heavenly joys. Finally, by being placed in such a way on the cross, He represented the serpent that Moses lifted up on the staff, so that those who were bitten by serpents might look upon it and be healed.

**Eusebius:** That is well explained; but let us consider, why did He wish to be buried with such care, wrapped in ointments, enclosed in a new tomb hewn from solid rock, with the entrance sealed and guarded by public officials?

**Archbishop:** For many reasons, one of which was to make it more evident and clear that He had truly risen, and He did not rise immediately; because if His death had been doubtful, so too would His resurrection have been, which He willed to be absolutely certain.

**Eusebius:** Since you have satisfied our questions, let us move forward. The fifth article is to *believe that He descended into hell and that He rose on the third day from the dead.*

**Antronio:** Tell us, did He suffer any harm there?

**Archbishop:** No, not at all.

**Antronio:** Then, why did He descend?

**Archbishop:** To deliver the souls of the holy fathers who had long awaited Him, and also so that, having broken the dominion of the devil, we might thereafter fight against the devil more securely.

**Antronio:** Why did He choose to rise again?

**Archbishop:** For three principal reasons: first, to give us certain hope of our own resurrection; second, so that we might know that He is immortal, and thus, more willingly place our hope for salvation in Him; and lastly, so that we, having died to sin through repentance and being buried with Jesus Christ through baptism, might be raised up by His grace to live a new kind of life.

**Antronio:** Indeed, these three reasons seem wonderfully sound to me. I wish I had everything you say written down!

**Eusebius:** It seems to me that since you find it so agreeable, you should write it down in your memory—or better yet, in your soul. But come now, let us not waste time.

The sixth article is to *believe that Jesus Christ ascended into heaven and is seated at the right hand of God the Father.*

**Archbishop:** That is indeed true, and it is what we all must believe.

**Eusebius:** Let us consider, why did He wish to leave the world?

**Archbishop:** So that we all might love Him spiritually and, at the same time, lift our souls to heaven. This way, no nation could boast of having Jesus Christ physically present in their land, nor could anyone love Him merely for His bodily presence, as it seems the Apostles did at one time.

**Eusebius:** Without a doubt, what you say is a very good and Christian reason, and may it please God that we who call ourselves Christians might learn not to place so much emphasis on these physical and external things, but to base our Christianity on what is spiritual and internal. God will bring this about in His time.

I wish to continue with my questions: the seventh article is to *believe that this same Jesus Christ will come from there to judge the living and the dead.* And I want you to tell me what you think about these comings.

**Archbishop:** I am pleased to do so. The first coming, according to the prophecies, was when Jesus Christ came in humility and lowliness to instruct our lives—that is, to show us how we ought to live if we wish to share in His glory, which He desires us to attain by virtue of His justice. There will also be a second coming, according to the prophecies, in which He will come in great majesty. All men, regardless of their status or nation, will stand before His presence, whether they like it or not, because all who have died from the beginning of the world until that day will be resurrected in an instant, and each one, clothed in his own body, will see the eternal judge. The blessed angels will be present there as faithful servants. The demons will also be present to be judged. And then, that divine judge, Jesus Christ, will pronounce from on high that immutable sentence, by which He will send to eternal torment all those who followed the banner of the devil, and He will take with Him all the righteous saints to enjoy the heavenly Kingdom together, free from all distress and labor. It is true that He did not wish to reveal to us the day of this coming; but all of this we Christians must believe, and we must also teach it to those we instruct.

**Antronio:** As for me, it feels like I'm hearing something out of a dream, because I knew no more about this than a simple board.

**Eusebius:** Very well.

The eighth article is to *believe in the Holy Spirit.* I am certain you will have wonderful things to tell us about this.

**Archbishop:** What I can tell you is that it is necessary for all of us to believe that the Holy Spirit is true God, together with the Father and the Son; and that these three persons are of one essence, meaning one and the same being. Since human reasoning alone is insufficient to persuade and comprehend this, the human understanding must be subjugated and submitted to the obedience of faith. It is by this same Spirit that we believe those who wrote the books of the Old and New Testaments were inspired; without His favor and grace, no one can attain eternal life or salvation.

**Eusebius:** Why is He called "Spirit"?

**Archbishop:** Because just as our bodies live through breath or air, so too are our souls given life through the secret inspirations attributed to the Holy Spirit.

**Eusebius:** Let us consider. Is it permissible to call the Father "Spirit"?

**Archbishop:** Yes, why not?

**Eusebius:** Because it seems to confuse the persons.

**Archbishop:** It does not. The Father is called Spirit because He is incorporeal, which is a quality common to all three persons according to the divine nature. But the third person is specifically called Spirit because it is attributed to Him to inspire and invisibly pass through our souls, just as air passes through the earth or through water.

**Antronio:** That is all a bit too lofty for me; you who understand it, sort it out among yourselves.

**Eusebius:** Even if you don't understand it now, don't worry; you will understand it one day. And since time is slipping away, you see that the ninth article is to *believe the Holy Catholic Church, which is the communion of saints.*

**Archbishop:** You are correct.

**Eusebius:** Then I want you to tell me why we don't say "in the Holy Church."

**Archbishop:** The reason for this is well noted by St. Cyprian, who explains that since we are only obligated to believe in God, the Apostles did not say "in the Holy Church," but simply "Holy Church."

**Antronio:** I don't quite understand that unless you explain it more clearly.

**Archbishop:** What St. Cyprian means is that we must place all our hope entirely in God and not in any creature. Since the Church is made up of people, who are creatures, it is not permissible for us to place our hope or trust in them. That is why the distinction is made.

**Antronio:** I see, but by that logic, one might say, "I believe in the Holy Church."

**Archbishop:** You should know that "Church" is a Greek word that means "congregation" or "assembly." So, what we are saying in this article is that we believe there exists in the world a church, which is an assembly of believers who believe in one God the Father, place all their trust in His Son, and are guided and governed by the Holy Spirit, who proceeds from both. Anyone who commits mortal sin separates themselves from this congregation. Thus, some people, as you seem to understand it, interpret the phrase "communion of saints" as a clarification of the first part. As if to say: the "Holy Catholic Church," meaning the assembly of saints, which is essentially a participation and communion among all the saints, who are the true Christians from the beginning of the world until the end. They share in one another's good works, much like the friendship and fellowship among the members of a body, so that they help one another. However, outside of this congregation, even one's own good works are of no benefit for eternal life unless they are reconciled and return to the holy congregation.

This is why the next article follows, which is to believe the forgiveness of sins; because outside of the Church I am speaking of, no one's sins are forgiven, even if they undergo severe penances or perform all works of mercy. And note that I say "in the Church," not in the church of heretics, but in the holy Church, meaning the one united with the Spirit of Jesus Christ. There is forgiveness of sins through baptism and afterward through penance and the keys that Jesus Christ gave to the Church. All of this must be known, believed, and taught in this way; and I am determined to ensure that it is done so in my archdiocese. For in this manner, the gross folly of many will be exposed, who rashly and foolishly claim that there are no more saints in the world; these fools fail to see that what they confess in the Creed, they deny in their conversations. This comes from not understanding what they profess to believe, and perhaps they do not know because no one has explained it to them.

**Antronio:** By the orders I have received, I have fallen into that folly many times without realizing it. But from now on, I will know better.

**Eusebius:** Yes, you will, I promise you. So now you should let me ask my question.

The eleventh article is to *believe in the resurrection of the flesh.* Tell us, what should we understand by "flesh"?

**Archbishop:** The human body, animated by a human soul.

**Antronio:** Since you answer so much to my satisfaction, tell me this: are we to believe that each soul will take up the same body it left behind?

**Archbishop:** Yes, without any doubt.

**Antronio:** It seems a difficult thing to believe that after a body has been reduced to dust, it could be raised again in its entirety.

**Archbishop:** Consider this, brother: if He who was able to create everything He desired from nothing, believe me, it will not be difficult for Him to restore what has been disfigured to its original form. Let us not trouble ourselves with disputing the manner in which this will be done, for it is enough for us to embrace this belief with faith rather than with human reasoning. Believe that He who promised this is so truthful that He cannot lie, and so powerful that He can accomplish whatever He wills in an instant.

**Antronio:** I am satisfied with that explanation; but tell me one more thing: what need will there be for bodies in that time?

**Archbishop:** Know, brother, that God wills that the whole person, both body and soul, should rejoice in glory with Jesus Christ, since here in the world both body and soul suffered affliction for Jesus Christ.

**Eusebius:** At the very least, you cannot complain that you are not satisfied with this; and since we have only the last article left, which is to believe eternal life, for charity's sake, explain it to us in great detail.

**Archbishop:** I will explain it as best I can. You must under-stand that in this life there are two kinds of death: one is of the body, which is common to both the good and the wicked; the other is of the soul. In the life to come, after the universal resur-rection, the good will have eternal life, both of body and soul. The body will be free from all fatigue, and being made spiri-tual, it will be governed by the spirit; and the soul, being free from all temptation, will enjoy without end the supreme good, which is God. On the other hand, the wicked will experience eternal death, both of body and soul, for their bodies will be immortal, so that they may be eternally tormented, and their souls, without any hope of mercy, will be perpetually afflicted by the sting of their sins.

**Antronio:** Truly, that pleases me greatly. Would that I could feel it as deeply as you can express it.

**Archbishop:** Look, brother, the ability to express things well is sometimes, as they say, a natural gift. But the ability to savor and feel them deeply, believe me, is a gift from God. I say this because if what I have said seems good to you and you desire the fruit of it, you must ask God for it; and ask not with luke-warm or cold prayers, but with great fervor, recognizing your need. For I want you to know that the fervor we have in prayer is directly proportional to the need we perceive in ourselves.

**Eusebius:** God is my witness that among the many explana-tions of the *Creed* I have heard, this one you have given here satisfies me the most. Therefore, I beg you, my lord, to tell me if you have learned it from some book.

**Archbishop:** I am pleased to answer you with great willingness. You must have heard of an excellent doctor, a true theologian who is still alive today, by the name of Erasmus of Rotterdam.

**Eusebius:** Yes, I have.

**Archbishop:** Have you read any of his works?

**Eusebius:** No, because some have advised me to avoid reading them.

**Archbishop:** Well, take my advice and leave those people to their foolishness; you should read and study the works of Erasmus, and you will see how much benefit you will gain. Moreover, you should know that among Erasmus's works, there is a little book of *Colloquies*, which he says he wrote so that children might learn both Latin and Christianity at the same time, as it deals with many Christian matters. Among these colloquies, there is one where the *Creed* is explained almost in the same way that I have explained it to you here. Do not be surprised that I have it so well memorized, as I have read it many times and with great attention.

**Eusebius:** I tell you truthfully, that aside from the authority of your person, which I hold in high regard, this explanation of the *Creed* alone will make me eager to read Erasmus, and I will never let his works out of my hands; this is what I intend to do from now on.

**Antronio:** By the habit of St. Peter, even though, based on the information from some of my friends, I was not well-disposed toward this Erasmus you speak of, from now on, I will regard him favorably, since you, my lord, praise him so highly. See how much good communication matters; but there is one condition—I do not understand Latin, so you will have to give me a copy of that colloquy, or whatever you call it.

**Archbishop:** I am willing to do that; I will make sure you receive a copy. But understand, honorable father, that such things are more necessary to be impressed and ingrained in the soul than simply written in books. I say this because I wish that you would place more value on having what has been said in your soul than in your chamber.

**Antronio:** Your advice is just what one would expect from such a person. I promise you that I will strive, as much as I can with the grace of Our Lord, to do what you say.

**Archbishop:** Do so, and I assure you that you will lose nothing by it. From this, you may also gather how you ought to explain the *Creed* to your students, and after one of them knows it, you should question them yourself, just as Eusebius has questioned me.

**Antronio:** I will do that as well.

**Eusebius:** Since the *Creed* has now been explained, it is fitting that we move forward. At the beginning, you said that the first thing a Christian child should be taught after the *Creed* are the Ten Commandments. Now you must tell us the reason for this.

**Archbishop:** I am pleased to do so. It is clear that after a person has learned in whom they should believe, and also what they should believe— which we have shown in the *Creed*— it is necessary for them to know the will of the One whom they now know and believe in. God declared this will in ancient times to the children of Israel by giving them the Ten Commandments, which we are still obliged to keep today. Jesus Christ, Our Lord, further clarified this will when He was present and conversed with us here in the world, as we may discuss later on. This is why I said what I did.

**Eusebius:** That was indeed well said. And since you are going to explain the Commandments to us, I would first like you to tell me why, in almost all of the Ten Commandments, God does not command us to do what He wants, but rather commands us not to do what He does not want. For example, why does He not say, "You shall worship only one God," but instead says, "You shall not worship other gods," and similarly with most of the others?

**Archbishop:** The full certainty of this matter lies in the wisdom of God; but with His grace, I will tell you what I once told another person who asked me the same question, and if you know of a better answer, feel free to share it. You should understand that human laws are established only to prevent us from doing something new that they forbid; but God's law is of a very different nature. Through it, we are not only warned about what we should do and not do in the future, but as St. Paul says, through it we come to understand the sinful wrongs we have committed against God. In this way, the law reveals to us how we are sinners, and this knowledge is the beginning of true justification. So, when I hear that it is God's will that I should not worship other gods, I become more aware of how I have sinned in this regard than if He had simply said, "Worship only one God." For when the law is stated in the first way, it seems to me as if the law is saying: "Oh, wretched man! Behold, I show you your wickedness. You should be such that you neither have other gods, nor take the name of your God in vain, nor kill, nor commit fornication— and yet here you are, far from this goodness, and instead, you are perverse."

**Eusebius:** By my faith, your answer is both subtle and deeply Christian. I have good hope that you will explain the rest in the same manner. And since we know that the first Commandment is, "You shall have no other gods," it remains for you to briefly explain and tell us what you wish all Christians to know about it, so that we may understand what we should teach them.

**Archbishop:** I am pleased to explain. First of all, since this commandment is broken by the sin of idolatry, it is essential to understand that there are primarily two types of idolatry: external and internal. External idolatry involves worshiping a piece of wood, a stone, an animal, or something similar, as some people did in ancient times according to the Old Testament and the writings of the pagans. This external idolatry stems from internal idolatry, which occurs when a person, out of fear of punishment or self-interest, refrains from outwardly worshiping these things, but inwardly places their love and trust in them.

It is of little value, in truth, to refrain from physically kneeling before honors, riches, or other creatures if we offer our hearts to them, which is the noblest part of a person. This is essentially worshiping God with the flesh, that is, with the outward body, while inwardly worshiping the creature with the spirit. God, recognizing this great affront we commit against Him, laments it in many parts of Sacred Scripture. For example, He says, "Israel, if you listen to Me, you will have no foreign god; you shall not worship a foreign god." It is as if He is saying to each of us: "Oh, sinful man, know that with your own strength and efforts, you will never reach such perfection that you do not worship foreign gods. For even if you do not outwardly worship statues, in your heart you still love creatures more than Me. So believe Me, you will not worship a foreign god when you listen to Me and, trusting in My words, believe them. Only this trust will remove and separate you from all greed and reliance on external things, and bring you to Me, who am your Creator."

**Antronio:** That is profound. Tell me, for charity's sake, how can one achieve this?

**Archbishop:** You should know that the faith and trust we place in Jesus Christ casts out all reliance on our own wisdom, righteousness, and virtue, because it teaches us that if Jesus Christ had not died for us, neither we nor any other creature could attain true happiness. From this understanding comes the disdain for all external things. Therefore, anyone who wishes to do what you ask must truly have this kind of trust. And so, when a Christian hears that Jesus Christ suffered for them, and believes it, a new trust is born within them, along with a certain love that is marvelously sweet. At the same time, all desire for external things fades, and a deep appreciation for Jesus Christ alone arises, knowing that He alone suffices, and from Him comes all things. For this reason, they love Him above all else.

It is clear, then, that only those who have complete faith, firm hope, and perfect love for Jesus Christ, our God and Redeemer, and who are completely detached from all attachment to external things, fulfill this first commandment. To achieve this, one undoubtedly needs the special grace of God.

**Antronio:** If you were to ask me whether I have any foreign gods, I would tell you that I do not, by no means.

**Archbishop:** I believe that you would say so, and yet this is where all the trouble lies: because we do not recognize our own faults, we do not seek the remedy for them, and thus we remain complacent in them. Let me ask you, for your own sake: are you so completely dead to all things and so secure in Jesus Christ that neither wealth makes you proud, nor poverty humbles you? Are you so unaffected by honors that they do not elevate you, nor by insults that they do not bring you down? Do you neither rejoice excessively in life nor despair in death? In short, are you so assured and at peace in all circumstances, whether good or bad, that you are confident in placing all your hope and trust in Jesus Christ?

**Antronio:** All that seems fine to me; but tell me, sir, what you say—is it not only for the perfect?

**Archbishop:** Indeed, it is for the perfect; that is to say, for Christians, and not for the unbelievers.

**Antronio:** Then, according to that, do you not make any distinction in the states of the militant Church, since you equate the commoner with the bishop in terms of perfection?

**Archbishop:** I am not speaking of that kind of perfection, but rather of Christian perfection, the kind in which the more one attains, the more perfect one becomes.

**Antronio:** So, according to your view, do all those who do not have this perfection go to hell?

**Archbishop:** I do not say that; but I do say that this is the goal or destination toward which we must all direct our efforts to achieve. And I also say that, of those who do not achieve it, only those are forgiven who, with sorrow of heart, recognize and confess that they are not as they ought to be, and those who, each day, strive to be such and to attain this perfection. And while they have not yet reached it, they say what is in the Lord's Prayer: "Forgive us our debts, as we also forgive our debtors." And as David says: "Create in me a clean heart, O God, and renew a right spirit within me." To these I say that their faults are forgiven through Jesus Christ, our Lord, in whom they believe. But as for those who, without fear and without care to improve in this path, sleep in complacency, they truly do not keep this Commandment. And I promise you that they will not excuse themselves by saying that it is only for the perfect, as you have said, for it is clear that it was not given for stones, but for men.

**Antronio:** Truly, I tell you, my flesh trembles at hearing you, and I do not know how to respond. What will happen, then, to the young people if I must tell them this?

**Archbishop:** That is great cowardice. Do not let your flesh tremble, but rather consider that, no matter how demanding this Commandment may be, God's grace is stronger, and with it, you can easily fulfill it. Considering this, ask God for it with humility, and I promise you He will not deny it. Then you will see how light and pleasant what now seems heavy and harsh truly is. And advise this same thing to all Christians, young and old.

**Antronio:** I will do as you say, but I would like you to tell me specifically who are those that sin against this Commandment.

**Archbishop:** Do not ask, out of love for me, that we spend our time on that here, for you will find a thousand confessors who can tell you, especially one of Teacher Ciruelo.

**Antronio:** I have seen it, but I would have liked to hear it from you.

**Archbishop:** Let that suffice for you, for all those who do not live with the simplicity and purity that we have mentioned break it.

**Eusebius:** I have greatly enjoyed hearing the priest's questions, and since this first commandment has now been well explained, let us move on to the second, which is: "You shall not take the name of the Lord your God in vain." Tell us what you think about it.

**Archbishop:** This commandment, like all the others, depends on the first, because whoever keeps the first keeps all the others.

**Eusebius:** If that is so, why are they set out as distinct?

**Archbishop:** To assist our blindness and dullness, for we do not even know what we ought to do, either outwardly or inwardly. Thus, the first commandment instructs the heart and the inner person in relation to God, and with this one, the mouth is instructed. Just as we sin against God in three ways— with the heart, the mouth, and through action—so there is a commandment for each. In the same way that one who sins in the heart does not sin by mouth or by deed, so too, one who sins in the heart cannot be justified either by mouth or by deed. Now, regarding our commandment, you must understand that, by commanding us not to take God's name in vain, we are given permission to take it in order to call upon Him, to praise Him, and to confess Him. As St. Paul says: "Whoever calls on the name of the Lord will be saved." Thus, we say that those who take it in vain are the sorcerers and those who practice similar arts, and those whose trade is gambling and cursing, and perhaps we might even include among these those who make use of certain incantations. For such people, as we see, do not take the name of God for the salvation of their souls or those of their neighbors, nor do they take it for the glory of God. Therefore, it seems they take it in vain, for those who take it without necessity and without cause take it in vain. The cause for which it is lawful to take it is for the glory of God and for the salvation of our souls, which are practically one and the same, and in truth, they are.

**Eusebius:** At the very least, you would not say that those who use such incantations with good intentions are sinning.

**Archbishop:** Why not?

**Antronio:** Because they say that the quality of the act depends on the intention. If their intention is good, why would the act be bad?

**Archbishop:** You are mistaken, for St. Paul does not hold that statement to be entirely true.

**Eusebius:** How so?

**Archbishop:** Because he says that, although the Jews' intention toward God was good, their persistence in obstinacy was a bad act. The reason why the act was bad is because their good intention was foolish.

**Eusebius:** That is well.

**Archbishop:** So you see; the same could be said of these people if they were still alive.

**Eusebius:** So, what you mean to say is that sometimes the intention is good, but the action is bad.

**Archbishop:** Yes, that is what I am saying. And if the authority of St. Paul is not enough for you, I will give you another from Jesus Christ, our Lord, who told His disciples that a time would come when those who killed them would believe they were offering service to God. Their intention, clearly, was good— to serve God— but it is equally clear that the act of killing the Apostles was evil. Why did this happen? Because their intention was misguided. Saul's intention in offering his sacrifice seemed good, but look at what he gained. David's intention in counting the people seemed good, and Uzzah's in trying to keep the ark from falling, and St. Peter's in offering to die with Jesus Christ— all seemed like good intentions. But because they lacked discretion in their good intentions, they were punished, as you see. Therefore, for an action to be truly good, the intention must be both good and guided by discretion.

**Eusebius:** You have made your point well; the charmers took a poor defender in me.

**Archbishop:** At the very least, as long as I live, I will make sure that those who practice such things in my Archdiocese will face a punishment that will be widely known. But leaving that aside, which is almost off-topic, I say that in regard to oaths, Jesus Christ, our Lord, wishing to remove the bad habit and vice of swearing from our hearts, said, as St. Matthew records: "You have heard it said to those of old, 'Do not swear falsely,' but I say to you, 'Do not swear at all.'" What Jesus Christ, our Lord, seems to mean by this is: It was commanded to the Jews that they should not perjure themselves, but they were allowed to swear as they wished. However, to you, I say, do not swear at all. Without a doubt, He wants to prevent anyone from swearing by their own will and without necessity. Therefore, He removes and forbids the voluntary act of swearing, so that no one, as far as it depends on them, should swear at all. Thus, if someone, of their own will and without any real purpose, says more than "yes" or "no," they go against this teaching of Jesus Christ. And let this suffice for the second Commandment.

**Eusebius:** Let that suffice, then, if you agree, and let us move on to the third Commandment, which is: "Remember to keep holy the Sabbath day." Explain this to us well, because it seems to me that either I do not understand it, or the common judgment on this matter is mistaken.

**Archbishop:** With God's grace, we will say what is necessary about it. First of all, you must recognize that in this Commandment, God commands us to rest, or rather, to cease from labor, so that the soul may rest when it fulfills the will of God. In doing so, we avoid offending God through sinful and servile works. Thus, these three Commandments prepare a person for God, like preparing clean material for building. That is, we are to rest in heart, in speech, and in action—in our outward, inward, and middle selves, which are the sensual, rational, and spiritual parts of the person—so that we may experience true rest.

**Antronio:** For your sake, my lord, do not go into such subtleties, for I do not understand them.

**Archbishop:** Very well, if that is your wish, I will speak more plainly. This Commandment, as you see, was given to the Jews to observe the Sabbath, and they understood it only in a literal sense, believing they fulfilled it simply by not working on that day.

**Eusebius:** To be honest, I would say that many of our Christians have hardly improved upon that understanding.

**Archbishop:** I see that, and it grieves me deeply. It is true that external works, even those that are good, were prohibited to the Jews because they symbolized sinful works. This is how we Christians must primarily understand it: God commands us that on holy days, we should be especially free from sin, for that is the true meaning of sanctifying the Sabbath—becoming holy on those days.

It hardly needs to be said how poorly this has been observed among Christians. But believe me, when I see gatherings of gossipers on feast days, whom David rightly calls "the seat of the pestilent," or groups of gamblers—some in the streets, others in the marketplaces—I am so filled with righteous anger that I could cry out in lament. Would it not be far better for those people to spend their time working in their fields than offending God? I do not know what else to say, except that I see Christian customs have fallen into such misery and blindness that what we think is keeping the holy days is actually breaking them. And on the very days when God commands us to become holy and devote ourselves entirely to Him, we instead become infernal and give ourselves wholly to Satan.

**Eusebius:** Since you feel so strongly about this, and since you are a prelate, why do you not remedy it?

**Archbishop:** Do you want me to tell you the truth? These things require a general remedy, and what troubles me is the lack of effort in bringing about that remedy. If it were up to me, I assure you that this issue would be quickly resolved. Indeed, you can see that it is already being addressed in my Archdiocese, and if I live, I will make sure that things change and move in a different direction than they have been.

**Archbishop:** But, leaving that aside, I say that a good Christian must think that every day is a holy day, and that on all days they must fulfill this precept and sanctify themselves—that is, improve their manner and way of living until they achieve full perfection, although this is especially true on Sundays and feast days. However, you must understand that in order to keep the Commandments in such a way that eternal life is gained through them, the person who keeps them must be free from mortal sin and possess charity, which is the perfect love of God. Without charity, even if the Commandments are outwardly observed, they are not fulfilled in the spirit for which they were instituted. And to have this charity, it is necessary that we ask God for it. Thus, my main point is that anyone who wishes to keep the Commandments properly must prioritize prayer above all else, and they will achieve more through this means than any other.

Now, it would be fitting to speak about the practices a Christian should engage in on such holy days, such as how to attend Mass and sermons, and other such matters. But we will leave those for another day.

**Eusebius:** You speak well, but I am amazed at how lightly you passed over the common opinion about these holy days, where people believe they have kept the day simply by not plowing or sowing, even though they spend the whole day playing games and engaging in worse activities.

**Archbishop:** That view is so widespread and more than common that there is no need to say more than what has already been said.

**Antronio:** I want to tell you a humorous story related to this that happened in my hometown when I was a boy, and hearing you speak has brought it to mind. You must know that on the Feast of the Transfiguration, there was a severe hailstorm, and it so happened that on that very day, a simple farmer sowed some turnips. His neighbors saw him and told others, and little by little, word spread throughout the city. Everyone concluded that the hailstorm was caused by the farmer's breaking of the holy day by sowing turnips. The local council gathered and sentenced him to pay for some candles and Masses and to provide a meal for the entire guild, which cost the poor man a great deal of money.

**Archbishop:** That is quite an amusing story. Certainly, that was a typical guild decision. I'm sure there were many in that city who spent the day gambling with cards and dice, or consorting with women, lying, gossiping, and engaging in other similar activities, yet they did not blame the hailstorm on them, but on the poor farmer. Oh, blessed be God for His great patience in tolerating so much evil and blindness! Truly, when I think about it, my heart breaks. I am not saying that the farmer did no wrong, but I lament the lack of respect people have for God's Commandments and the false and misguided judgments we make in these matters.

**Eusebius:** Well, let's leave that aside and move on to the fourth Commandment, which is: "Honor your father and your mother." Since it is getting late, it will be enough for you to briefly tell us what we need to know about it.

**Archbishop:** Very well. You should know that this Commandment must be understood both spiritually and literally. Spiritual honor toward parents means giving them your heart, voluntary obedience, and proper respect, holding them in high regard. Literally, it means honoring them with outward ceremonies and providing for their needs if they are lacking, and ensuring they are well cared for in times of necessity. If they lack, it is the children's duty to seek out what they need through honest work. I urge you to emphasize this to everyone.

Indeed, it is also important to emphasize that parents must fulfill their obligations toward their children. The most essential duty is to instruct them in the faith and in good and holy customs, teaching them to fear God rather than men. Parents should raise their children in such a way that the children do not think they are merely respecting and fearing their parents as people, but rather, they understand that they are honoring and fearing God through their parents. In this way, they should recognize that if they offend their parents, they are not only offending them but also offending God.

It is also part of this Commandment to teach how women should be subject to their husbands and the proper way in which this subjection should take place, which the Apostle teaches well by providing an example of Sarah in one of his letters. Likewise, this Commandment involves teaching how husbands should treat their wives, which St. Peter explains very well. Additionally, it is necessary to teach how servants should obey their masters, as this too is related to this Commandment. According to Sacred Scripture, the servants of Naaman called him "father," showing that servants must honor their masters, both outwardly and inwardly, just as children should honor their parents. This is what St. Peter means. Masters must also be instructed not to be tyrannical with their servants but to remember that both they and their servants have the same Heavenly Father and Lord. They should treat their servants not as slaves, but as brothers.

Furthermore, you must tell your children that they are obligated to obey, respect, and honor their superiors, priests, princes, and those who administer justice, as they are appointed by God. Finally, you should instruct them that both children and adults must honor and respect their teachers and elders, both in age and in dignity. Even nature itself teaches this, as we naturally refer to an older man as "father" or "uncle" and an older woman as "mother" or "aunt."

The Jews had this Commandment, like the others, corrupted and distorted in countless ways. They taught their children that whatever they gave to their parents was better offered to the temple, and they had no shortage of words to justify their wickedness.

**Antronio:** By my life, you have spoken directly to me, for I have certainly sinned in this matter myself.

**Archbishop:** I wish it were only you, but unfortunately, this is a widespread illness among many. May Our Lord, by His infinite goodness, remedy it, for no one else can. What you must particularly advise your children is to help their parents as much as they can with their possessions, if their parents are in need; then, to help their relatives, and after that, those who are in need. They should prioritize helping those they see as more Christian, as the Apostle advises. Finally, they should help their neighbors whenever they see them in need. To conclude this Commandment, I say that the first honor is owed to God, as our Father from whom we receive so many blessings; then, to our own parents; next, to those who hold positions of authority and jurisdiction, both in the Church and in secular society; and finally, to the elderly, to maintain Christian peace and harmony. Let that suffice for this Commandment.

**Eusebius:** Let it suffice, since you deem it so. Now tell us about the fifth Commandment, which is, "You shall not kill."

**Archbishop:** Before we proceed, I want to show you the marvelous order that these Commandments follow. You should note that the first four Commandments seem directed toward God and His representatives, who are each person's parents. The remaining six are directed toward our neighbor, and within them, there is a remarkable order. They begin with the most grievous offenses and move to the lesser ones: the greatest harm is to kill a person, followed by committing adultery, then stealing. And because those who cannot harm with deeds might use their tongue to harm others, false testimony follows. For those who do not sin in any of these ways but still desire in their hearts what they cannot bring to fruition, the last two Commandments address this.

This Commandment, like the others, was corrupted by the Pharisees. They claimed that one did not sin against it unless they killed someone with their own hands. Because of this, and other similar distortions, Jesus Christ said: "Unless your righteousness exceeds that of the Pharisees and the scribes, you will not enter the kingdom of heaven." The reason was that the Pharisees interpreted the law literally and not according to the intention of God, who gave the law. For this reason, Jesus, desiring to clarify the Commandment, said, according to St. Matthew: "You have heard it said to those of old, 'You shall not kill.' But I tell you, anyone who is angry with his brother..." From this, it becomes clear that we are obligated by this Commandment not to harbor any anger or resentment against our neighbors, nor to speak anything behind their backs or to their face that could harm them.

**Antronio:** By that reasoning, those who consider it a point of pride, or even their duty, to continuously mock and ridicule others have something to reflect on.

**Archbishop:** And that is precisely what pains me. I see many such people constantly—those who, with a rosary hanging from their belts and a prayer book tucked into their sleeves, attending Mass daily, think that if they were to tally their deeds with God, they would come out in good standing.

**Eusebius:** No doubt about that. I receive confession from many such people myself, and I see the truth in what you say. They believe that if their rosary beads are blessed, or if they wear some little token of the Trinity, then, in their eyes, they can save not only their own souls but even the souls of their companions!

**Archbishop:** Because to talk about this would require more patience than I usually have, and it's excessive here, it's best to leave it and return to our subject.

You should know that this Commandment is so deep that no one can fully keep it without grace. The truth is, if each person examines themselves thoroughly, few will find that they don't falter in this area. Therefore, anyone who wishes to keep this Commandment should strive as much as possible to love everyone sincerely, or better yet, pray to God for the grace to attain this love. And let no one presume to say that they bear no ill will toward anyone, for without a doubt, a person who does not sin in this Commandment is remarkably peaceful and humble. That spiritual anger, which this Commandment forbids, is so deep that, although it may not manifest outwardly in words or actions, it often remains deeply rooted within the innermost part of the heart.

**Antronio:** Well then, tell me, how will I know if I have hatred against my neighbor or not?

**Archbishop:** I will explain. When you recognize in yourself that your spirit is so calm and subdued that, even if everything you have, including your life, were taken from you, you would bear no hatred against the one who took it, then you can be sure that you are free from this sin.

**Antronio:** What? Must a person be so pure that they cannot even harbor resentment for the wrongs done to them?

**Archbishop:** Yes, that is what I mean, because nothing impure can enter the kingdom of heaven. But listen further—it is not enough that a Christian remains unmoved by anger in such a situation. The Christian must also speak well of those who speak ill of them, do good to those who persecute them, and pray for them. Finally, they must give thanks to God in adversities just as in times of prosperity, believing that all such trials come as a consequence of their sins, and therefore they should hate the sin and not the punishment that is inflicted because of it.

**Antronio:** I don't know what to say, except that I would think such a thing is only for the perfect.

**Archbishop:** You are correct, for to attain what I describe, one must be perfect. But it is important that everyone knows this, so that those who fall short of it may recognize that they are not perfect. By knowing this, they will understand that they are not fully keeping this Commandment, and thus they should pray continually to God to transform them from being imperfect to being perfect, for every Christian must strive for this perfection. To conclude this Commandment, I will say that we should note that it applies from the lesser, more internal sins to the more outward and manifest ones. That is why I have not spoken much about those who, through speech, action, or counsel, cause someone's death.

**Eusebius:** We understand that. What you have said is sufficient. Now that this Commandment is explained, let us move on to the sixth Commandment, which is: "You shall not commit adultery." But I would like you to say little about it, as I know you are reluctant to speak of it because of your modesty.

**Archbishop:** Indeed, you are correct. But I will speak of it with the understanding that you already know the various ways in which this Commandment is broken through sins of the flesh.

**Eusebius:** You are right.

**Archbishop:** Then know this: because the Pharisees had also corrupted the understanding of this Commandment, Jesus Christ, as St. Matthew records, sought to clarify it. He said that whoever looks at a woman with lust has already committed adultery with her in his heart. Therefore, according to these words of Jesus Christ, we can identify four ways in which one can sin against this Commandment: through desire, through gestures, through words, and through actions. It is not necessary to specify them here, as I know I am speaking to those who understand this.

There exists another form of adultery which, though less perceptible, is all the more dangerous. This occurs when the soul of the Christian—who ought to love God alone, placing all thought and affection in Him—turns inward to love itself, or directs affection to any other entity apart from God. Oh, how immense is this adultery, and how grievous the injury and affront that the Christian soul inflicts upon God! The soul, which should be entirely dedicated to Him, instead seeks the world, pursuing honors, wealth, lordships, reputation, favors, privileges, and other such things. Indeed, to fully uphold this commandment, it is necessary to keep vigilant in prayer before God, night and day.

**Eusebius:** I must say that you are entirely correct and that your words are very pleasing to me.

**Antronio:** As for myself, I feel as though I am beginning to understand that until now, I have not truly known what it means to be a Christian. Blessed be God, who has now revealed it to me.

**Eusebius:** That is well; I assure you that you will express this understanding even more sincerely as you continue to comprehend it more deeply.

Now, let us move on: the seventh commandment is, "Thou shalt not steal."

**Archbishop:** That is indeed correct, and it must be understood in two ways. First, in the literal sense; thus, we can say that here, stealing is explicitly forbidden. The Jews understood it in this sense alone, and hence, anyone who did not steal regarded themselves as holy. The second understanding is spiritual, in accordance with the principal intention of God who gave us this commandment. Therefore, all forms of greed reigning in the heart are here forbidden, to the extent that it is impossible to fulfill this commandment except for one who is "poor in spirit."

**Eusebius:** Now then, whom do you call "poor in spirit"?

**Archbishop:** It is one who neither wants nor desires anything beyond what they have and who has so fully removed their attachment to even what they possess that, should it be taken away, they would suffer no distress.

**Antronio:** Then, according to this, does this commandment also require us to avoid covetousness?

**Archbishop:** Do not doubt it. To fulfill this commandment, it is essential to mortify that insatiable beast of avarice, which the Apostle describes as the root of all evil, and which he also calls idolatry. Beyond this, we break this commandment by stealing from God what is His. This happens when we give to creatures the reverence, love, and fear that are rightfully His alone. Furthermore, were we to scrutinize whether a man pays his due to his soul, whether children give what is owed to their parents, parents to their children, servants to their masters, and masters to their servants, it would be an endless inquiry. And if we were to examine ourselves as clergy, I assure you we would find much that astonishes. But my main point, as I have said, is that only the spiritual man can truly uphold this commandment, as well as all the others.

**Antronio:** By your life, please tell me whom you call a "spiritual man." Do you perhaps mean monks or clerics?

**Archbishop:** You are greatly mistaken; neither monks nor clerics alone. Do you know, father, who the spiritual man is? He is the one who perceives and delights in spiritual matters, finding joy and rest in them, while disregarding and even despising physical and external matters as lesser things. In short, he is the one who places all his love in God, lives by it, and preserves the grace of the Holy Spirit, whether he be young, married, cleric, or monk.

**Antronio:** Shall I tell you, sir? This religion of yours is exceedingly narrow, for in that way very few can keep God's commandments.

**Archbishop:** I admit that few keep them, yet I also confess that among those who do not keep them are those who, recognizing their shortcomings, humble themselves before God and strive to keep them as best they can. They confess their sins, do penance for the failings they have fallen into, and hope to obtain forgiveness through the blood of Jesus Christ.

**Eusebius:** What has been said suffices to explain this commandment. Now, tell us your understanding of the eighth commandment, which is, "Thou shalt not bear false witness against thy neighbor."

**Archbishop:** In this commandment, God commands us not to harm our neighbors, whether by damaging their reputation or honor. Against this, countless types of people sin: the gossipers, slanderers, liars, deceivers, and even teachers who instruct their students with falsehoods, as well as preachers who, rather than presenting doctrine as they understand and should understand it, present it in a way that suits them best. To achieve their aims, all of these must raise a thousand false testimonies. Among them, without any doubt, the gravest guilt lies with those preachers who, to make Scripture say what they desire, twist and corrupt it, making it say what it does not intend. There are also those who, to incite the people toward questionable devotions, preach in pulpits and outside them about dubious miracles, recounting stories and events that are false and deceitful, all for the sake of their accursed and diabolical interests, of which the Apostle says, "their god is their belly." But because these people and others like them are entirely dedicated to serving the world, their sole occupation is to satisfy their carnal desires; and they have only the name of Christians, we ought not waste our time speaking of them, nor give them any attention except to pray to God to lead them out of their vile and corrupt ways and grant them hearts obedient to His most holy will. My wish is that all church leaders would be such that, understanding well the evil in these matters, they would punish it decisively so that at least by necessity, they might compel virtue.

**Eusebius:** In all that you have said, you are entirely correct; I trust in God that you will address these matters accordingly. Now, tell us about the ninth commandment, which states: You shall not covet your neighbor's wife.

**Archbishop:** If you recall, we expounded upon this commandment when discussing the sixth. For the same principle that we stated there, as expressed by Jesus Christ in His explanation of that commandment, applies here as well.

**Eusebius:** That is indeed true, but nevertheless, please elaborate further.

**Archbishop:** I do not know what else to say except that God desires us to be entirely free from all sin, pure both outwardly and inwardly. Thus, He is not content merely to command in the sixth commandment that we refrain from committing adultery; rather, He adds this commandment to ensure that we uproot and eradicate the very source of adultery—namely, concupiscence. For just as we recognize that, in order to prevent a wicked tree from growing back once it has been cut down, it is necessary to remove all of its roots, so too, if we do not wish for the tree of adultery to sprout again after being cut down, we must remove the roots from which it originates, which are the corrupt desires leading to sin.

**Eusebius:** That is as well stated as everything else you have explained. But let us proceed further—tell us about the final commandment: You shall not covet your neighbor's possessions.

**Archbishop:** We also discussed this commandment extensively when addressing the seventh, in which we spoke of greed. As we noted, Saint Paul states that greed is the root of all evil and that those who desire to become rich fall into temptation and the snares of the devil. In addition to all that we have said, I wish to offer you a valuable and subtle insight that will help you grasp all of this concisely: the prohibitions in these commandments necessarily imply affirmative injunctions, which further clarify their meaning.

For instance, the first commandment, You shall have no other gods before Me, is affirmed in the positive sense as follows: You shall worship one God alone and love Him exclusively.

The second commandment, You shall not take the name of the Lord your God in vain, is affirmed positively as: You shall invoke and glorify the name of the Lord with reverence and fear, bless Him with humility and awareness of your own insignificance, and swear by His name only when necessity demands it.

The third commandment, Remember to keep the Sabbath day holy, means in its affirmative sense: You shall refrain from servile work on that day, ceasing from all physical and spiritual labor. Here, spiritual labor refers to sin, for there is no greater toil for the soul than being separated from God.

The fourth commandment, Honor your father and mother, is self-evidently affirmative in nature.

The fifth commandment, You shall not kill, is affirmed positively as: Be peaceful, gentle in heart, patient, calm, and serene; and treat your neighbor as you would wish to be treated.

The sixth commandment, You shall not commit adultery, can also be expressed in its affirmative sense: Be chaste, self-disciplined, temperate, sober, and modest—and do so with a sincere and joyful heart.

The seventh commandment, You shall not steal, is likewise affirmed by the exhortation: Be poor in spirit, content with what you have, and modest in your desires.

The eighth commandment, You shall not bear false witness, is positively expressed as: Cultivate true friendship with your neighbor, excusing and defending him, and ultimately treating him as you would wish to be treated.

The ninth and tenth commandments, You shall not covet your neighbor's wife, nor his possessions, are likewise made clear through their affirmative expressions: Harbor goodwill toward your neighbors from the depths of your heart, desire their well-being, and do them no harm.

From all that has been said, we may clearly deduce that the Ten Commandments have been thoroughly elucidated by Jesus Christ, our God and Lord, as well as by His Apostles, who teach that we must possess faith, hope, charity, obedience, reverence, humility, meekness, peace, patience, modesty, chastity, poverty, goodness, kindness, and, ultimately, that we must love one another.

To attain all these virtues—without which one cannot fulfill God's law—divine grace is absolutely necessary. Without His favor, we can accomplish nothing that is truly good. For this reason, Saint Paul declares that the law is spiritual, meaning that in order to fulfill it, one must possess the Spirit; or rather, that only the spiritual man is able to keep it.

**Eusebius:** Two important questions remain regarding these commandments—questions I have long desired to understand. First, why did God give us commandments that, as you have said, we cannot fulfill by our own human strength alone? And second, why is the commandment to love God and one's neighbor not explicitly included among the Ten Commandments, when we see that in the New Testament, these are often declared to be the first and second greatest commandments?

**Archbishop:** I will gladly explain what I know regarding both matters. Concerning the first question, you must understand that Saint Paul states that the law was given to reveal sin—that is, to show us how, in many ways, we sin daily. From the sin of our first father, Adam, we have inherited this corrupt inclination toward evil. However, we were unaware of this inclination until the law was given, which exposed our sinful nature to us. The law also revealed what is good, but it was not sufficient to empower us to do what is right. Instead, it served only to make us aware of our misery, weakness, and sinful disposition. This awareness, in turn, was meant to humble us before God and lead us to recognize ourselves as sinners. Thus, Saint Paul says that he would not have known concupiscence if the law had not said, You shall not covet. This is the function of the law. Then, with the coming of Jesus Christ, He granted us the Spirit by which we are enabled to perform the good that the law had revealed but could not empower us to accomplish. Thus, we come to understand that what we could not achieve by our own strength and efforts, we can fulfill through the grace of Christ. By experience, we learn that, by our fallen nature, we are incapable of true righteousness, but through the favor of Christ, we can accomplish and obey all that is good. Consequently, we abandon all confidence in our own strength and learn to place our complete trust in divine grace and favor. In this knowledge, we willingly entrust all our affairs to God, assured that He will not fail us. This was necessary so that mankind would humble itself before God, and through this humility, attain eternal glory. For, as I have mentioned before, God willed that we should gain salvation through humility, since the fallen angels lost it through pride. Thus, this is my response to your first question. And if you consider it carefully, from what has been said, you may also deduce the fundamental distinction between the Law and the Gospel.

**Eusebius:** That is very well explained; I am fully satisfied with your response to the first question. Now, let us proceed to the second.

**Archbishop:** In truth, I do not have a definitive answer to give you on this matter. However, I do know that, according to the Gospel of Matthew, a doctor of the Law once asked Jesus Christ, "Which is the greatest commandment in the Law?" To which He responded: "You shall love the Lord your God with all your heart, with all your soul, and with all your will. This is the first and greatest commandment. But the second is like it: You shall love your neighbor as yourself." He then added: "On these two commandments hang all the Law and the Prophets." From these words, we may infer two things. First, in calling these commandments the first and second, Christ is not referring to their numerical order within the Decalogue—for we do not find them explicitly listed among the Ten Commandments—but rather to their dignity or preeminence. Second, in stating that all the Law and the Prophets depend upon these two commandments, He implies that the Ten Commandments themselves are contained within them, just as the truth of the Law is contained in love.

**Eusebius:** How so?

**Archbishop:** I shall explain. The first three commandments, which pertain to God, are encompassed within the command to love God. For it is evident that one who loves God will worship Him alone, will not take His name in vain but rather glorify and praise it, and will observe the holy days in His honor. These three commandments are traditionally referred to as belonging to the first table of the Law. The remaining seven, which belong to the second table, pertain to love for one's neighbor. It is self-evident that one who loves his neighbor will neither steal from him nor kill him, nor commit any of the transgressions that these commandments prohibit. Thus, Saint Paul rightly states that he who loves fulfills the Law, and elsewhere, that love is the fulfillment of the Law.

**Eusebius:** Truly, my lord, your wisdom and discernment surpass all that I have encountered or discussed before.

**Antronio:** You speak most truly. However, for my own understanding, I would ask that his lordship summarize these two commandments in just a few words.

**Archbishop:** In all honesty, I do not know what further explanation you require beyond what we have already discussed, both in the first article of the Creed and in the first commandment—if, indeed, you recall our previous discussion.

**Antronio:** Yes, I do recall it well. But I am certain that you still have something more of value to share with us.

**Archbishop:** Your zeal is commendable; it is necessary, then, that I obey you and fulfill your request. You must understand that the human heart cannot help but love something. In this, there is no middle ground: either one loves oneself and, for personal gain and interest, all things; or one loves God, and in God and for His glory, all things. Now, knowing that if man loves himself with this disordered love, he will never be able to do anything truly good in God's sight, nor will he be able to submit to His law or refrain from following his irrational appetites—since self-love blinds him—God, desiring our salvation, commands us to love Him above all things. For, as He is supremely good, by loving Him above all things, we love all that is good and abhor all that is evil. Thus, moved by the love we have for Him, we delight in fulfilling His law, doing so willingly and joyfully. In this way, we experience the profound truth of what our Lord Jesus Christ declared: that His yoke is easy, and His burden is light. Conversely, those who love themselves find everything burdensome and heavy. Therefore, when you hear someone say that obeying God's law is difficult and that the doctrine of Jesus Christ is hard to bear—even if you witness that person performing miracles—believe me when I say that they lack this love. You must apply this same test to yourself daily, and you will always find that, no matter how righteous you may perceive yourself to be, you still fall short—indeed, greatly so. And if ever it seems to you that nothing is lacking, rest assured that everything is lacking. We may also assess the extent to which we possess this love by examining our hearts: Are we firmly resolved to lose wealth, honor, and reputation, and to suffer a thousand deaths rather than consent to a mortal sin? If we find that our hearts are steadfast in this resolution, then there is good reason to hope that we have attained some measure of this love. However, do not believe that you truly possess it until you have thoroughly tested it through experience. If, on the other hand, we do not find ourselves with this firm determination, we may be certain that we are lovers of ourselves rather than lovers of God. In such a case, we must courageously turn to Jesus Christ and fervently implore His divine grace and favor so that we may attain what we recognize to be lacking in us. If we earnestly hope that He will grant it to us, we may be certain that we shall not be left without it.

**Antronio:** Say what you will, but I must confess that keeping this commandment is an exceedingly difficult task.

**Archbishop:** Consider, Father Curate, how mistaken you are! I assure you that I can truthfully say this: it seems to me that I owe God far more for having commanded me to love Him in this manner than He owes me for my love toward Him. Indeed, I say even more: every time I reflect upon this commandment, I am drawn anew to God with fresh affection. I do not know whether I should say it, but at times I feel that I am more indebted to God for the grace He has shown in commanding me to love Him than for the fact that He created me as a man and not as a brute animal. To conclude, I say that in order to keep this commandment, it is not enough for man merely to refrain from self-love; rather, he must utterly despise himself, his possessions, his pleasures, and delights, and in all things mortify his earthly desires. Whoever lacks this disposition should know that he is not truly keeping this commandment.

**Antronio:** By my faith, you have startled me more with this last statement than with anything else you have said thus far. It is evident that you speak as one both experienced and learned, so much so that you lack nothing in understanding. Since this is the case, tell us something about love for one's neighbor.

**Archbishop:** Truly, I do not know what else to say, except that in this commandment, as in the previous one, my soul contemplates the supreme goodness and benevolence of God in two ways. The first is that He commands me to do what I am naturally bound to do. To me, it seems that He gives this command so that, if I fulfill it, He may have cause to bestow upon me the glory that He has prepared exclusively for those who obey Him in this life. Can you conceive of any generosity or magnificence that could compare to this? The second way is that God has placed before me an avenue through which I may demonstrate my love for Him: by commanding me to love my neighbor. Through this commandment, He obliges me never to think, speak, or do anything that might harm my neighbor. Beyond this, He requires that I always, to the best of my ability, seek my neighbor's welfare, promote his good, and protect him from harm—even to the point of sometimes setting aside my own personal interests for his benefit. These are the very things you must teach and impress upon all those whom you instruct, regardless of their status. For in my archdiocese, I have decreed that this be done in the same manner, and, God willing, it shall soon come to pass. If anyone should ask you, "Who is my neighbor?" tell them that it is every man, whether Christian or not. It is true, as Saint Paul teaches, that we are more obligated to do good to those who love God most and whom we see as most obedient to Him.

**Antronio:** I am greatly astonished by what you say. Does not God Himself declare that well-ordered charity begins with oneself?

**Archbishop:** I have heard this said, but I do not know that God has ever spoken it; rather, it is something devised by men who love themselves excessively. Even if this saying could be given a proper meaning, they insist on interpreting it in the worst possible sense. Do you not see how ridiculous this rule is? It is not a principle of charity, but of carnality. You are gravely mistaken if you think this to be true.

**Antronio:** From now on, I shall no longer believe it. Indeed, I think that if I converse with you often, you will make me into an entirely different man.

**Archbishop:** It is Jesus Christ who will accomplish this, through His infinite goodness. Let this be our final conclusion: these two commandments are so closely connected and inseparably united that it is impossible to observe one without the other. For he who loves God understands that it is God's will that he love his neighbor. Since his sole desire is to please God, he therefore loves his neighbor and, by doing so, fulfills the entire law of God. Truly, I do not understand how some men, who never display any sign of this love in their lives, can consider themselves superior Christians merely because of certain ceremonies and devotions they have invented. What is even more lamentable is that when they see someone who does not adopt or venerate their cold and empty devotions—though that person clearly lives according to the law of God—they do not even regard him as a Christian. This is undoubtedly the justice of the Pharisees, who exalt their outward works while belittling and disregarding the inward devotion of others. Leave this matter to me, for if God grants me life, I will take action in such a way that the wicked will be left in awe and the righteous will rejoice.

**Eusebius:** May God grant it to you, along with His grace, so that you may fulfill what you have spoken. Since you have so excellently explained the commandments to us, it is necessary that we proceed further, so that there may be time for all things.

**Archbishop:** You speak well; let us now leave aside the commandments and see what else you wish to learn.

**Eusebius:** I recall that, at the beginning, you told us that after learning the commandments, it is fitting for a Christian to study the three chapters of Matthew—chapters five, six, and seven. Tell us, then, what is the reason that you consider this to be necessary?

**Archbishop:** I am pleased to explain. The soul that is already instructed in the faith, as I believe I have told you, and that already believes what must be believed concerning God, must then learn the will of God so that it may act according to its faith. Part of this is revealed in the Ten Commandments, and part is found in these chapters of Matthew. For this reason, I deem it necessary that every Christian learn them promptly. In these chapters, Christ teaches the nature of the blessedness that one can attain in this life, how the righteous are those whom the world persecutes, and how the wicked are the persecutors. He commands us to forgive one another's offenses, to avoid litigiousness, to refrain from repaying evil with evil, but rather to return good for evil. He instructs that if someone strikes us on one cheek, we should turn the other to receive another blow; if anyone seeks to sue us for our cloaks, we should yield our tunics as well rather than engage in litigation. Moreover, He commands us to give to those who ask, to lend to those who seek a loan, and to love our enemies. In these passages, He teaches us how to fast, how and what to pray, and many other similar matters. From them, we learn to disdain worldly honors and wealth, in which the common people suppose blessedness resides. We learn to bear patiently the insults and reproaches inflicted upon us by others, to be humble, peaceful, and composed. We learn to avoid hypocrisy, to shun avarice, and instead to cultivate generosity and liberality toward all. It is not only necessary that every Christian know these teachings by heart, but also that they deeply impress them upon their soul before it becomes corrupted by false and pernicious opinions.

**Antronio:** But, my lord, do you not see that these teachings are merely advisory?

**Archbishop:** That, by grievous sin, is the claim of those who seek a pretext for their wickedness. I indeed believe that they are counsel, yet such counsel that without it, perfect Christian peace and tranquility cannot be maintained. Since this is the case, I implore you not to diminish their importance by calling them mere counsel; rather, since you see how vital they are, teach them to all, for they will do no harm.

**Antronio:** I am content with this, but on the condition that you, my lord, provide them to me in the vernacular.

**Archbishop:** I shall gladly do so, and even at once, for in order that they may be taught throughout my archbishopric, I have already arranged for them to be translated into the vernacular.

**Antronio:** At the very least, if you send all those who come to deal with you away with such teachings as you have given me, none will depart dissatisfied. And since we have the time, I entreat you, by your life, to instruct us on what ought to be taught concerning the seven deadly sins.

**Archbishop:** To tell you the truth, this is a matter I do not willingly discuss, for scrutinizing sins is of little benefit to the wicked and tends to breed undue scruples in the righteous. However, since I must comply with your request, I shall share what seems fitting to me. You may take from it what you will.

**Eusebius:** First, tell us, why was the number seven assigned to these sins?

**Archbishop:** Saint John Chrysostom explains that just as the Israelites fought against seven kings to obtain the Promised Land, so too must the Christian battle against these seven vices in order to enter his Promised Land, which is blessedness.

**Eusebius:** By my salvation, that saying is worthy of the one who uttered it. Now, tell us the rest.

**Archbishop:** First of all, you must know that these seven deadly sins are prohibited within the Ten Commandments, as I shall soon demonstrate. Thus, whoever keeps the commandments will inevitably avoid falling into any of these sins. The first sin is pride, which manifests in two forms: externally, when a person takes pride in material possessions, and internally, when one boasts of spiritual gifts. For this reason, pride is prohibited in the First Commandment, which, as we have already discussed, commands us not to have any other gods. This means that we should trust in, take delight in, and find satisfaction and joy in nothing but God alone. You can see how pride sometimes leads a person to take excessive pride in wealth, strength, clothing, power, honor, nobility, and social standing. Internally, it fosters confidence in one's own wisdom, knowledge, intellect, righteousness, virtue, and holiness, thereby attributing to these things what rightfully belongs to God. Moreover, pride brings with it two additional vices: first, it makes the presumptuous person hold himself in excessive esteem; and second, it leads him to despise, scorn, and detest others. For this reason, pride also encompasses vainglory.

Thus, when the proud recognize some virtue within themselves, they do not give thanks to God for it nor attribute it to Him as they should, but rather ascribe it to themselves. In this way, they fulfill what Saint Paul declares: "Professing themselves to be wise, they became fools." You must recognize this sin as particularly dangerous, for it is subtle and often goes unnoticed. Since it does not manifest outwardly in a tangible form, we make little effort to rid ourselves of it, failing even to recognize its presence. Consequently, it accompanies many people to the grave, as is evident from the numerous last wills and testaments we see daily, filled with vanity and pride—an unfortunate and pitiable sight. The truth is, I place a good portion of the blame for this on confessors.

**Antronio:** I am astounded by what you have said. Since you have exposed the wound, I implore you, out of charity, to provide the remedy. Tell me how I might flee from this sin and teach others to do the same. And please, do the same for the rest.

**Archbishop:** I am willing. The first and most effective remedy is to sincerely recognize your inclination toward this sin and to grieve over it before God, constantly sighing in prayer and asking for His grace to subdue it and extinguish its hold on you. Additionally, you will find it greatly beneficial always to compare yourself with those who are greater and more virtuous than yourself, rather than with those who are inferior. Furthermore, it will help you to focus more on your faults and weaknesses than on your virtues and strengths.

**Eusebius:** Indeed, if the wound has been thoroughly exposed, the remedy is more than sufficient for its healing. Since this is the case, tell us now about avarice.

**Archbishop:** Saint Paul calls avarice "the root of all evil" because those who seek to become rich fall into the snares of the devil and into many vain, unprofitable, and harmful desires. This sin is prohibited in two commandments—namely, the seventh and the last—and even in the first. For in commanding us not to steal, God also commands us not to be avaricious, just as He does when He forbids us from coveting our neighbor's possessions. There is little need to elaborate on the first point, for it is evident that the avaricious person desires something apart from God, thereby violating the First Commandment. This is even more clearly stated by Saint Paul, who declares that the greedy are idolaters. I consider this sin to be particularly dangerous for the same reason as pride: because it is a sin of the soul, it remains unseen. And since it is not seen, it is not recognized; and since it is not recognized, we make no effort to eradicate it. To be frank, I would not dare to say that I myself am free from avarice, nor would I advise anyone to believe himself free from it, no matter how detached he may seem. Rather, I will always acknowledge my own inclination toward it, making it a cause for lament before God and a reason to confess my misery. At the same time, I take comfort in Christ's words: "Blessed are those who mourn, for they shall be comforted."

**Eusebius:** Your reasoning is so thoroughly Christian that there is nothing more to ask. Since you are so adept at both diagnosing and healing, tell us now about lust.

**Archbishop:** Saint Paul instructs that this sin should not even be named among Christians—and rightly so, for it is so base and beastly. It is explicitly prohibited in the Sixth Commandment, which forbids adultery, about which, I believe, we have already spoken sufficiently. The remedy for this sin is temperance in food and drink, maintaining chaste and honorable conversations, and fleeing from idleness, which is the mother of all vice and sin. When teaching children about this sin, say as little as possible, and whatever is said should be framed in such a way that they will abhor it before they even come to understand it.

**Antronio:** I will follow your instruction in this and in all else.

**Eusebius:** Very well. Now tell me about wrath.

**Archbishop:** I assure you that if we examine this matter thoroughly, there is much to be said, for, if I am not mistaken, there are few who are entirely free from it—some more, some less. We have already spoken about this sin in relation to the Fifth Commandment; now we shall expand upon it a little further and, with God's grace, provide every Christian with the means to guard against it. To clarify, wrath is any thought, word, or action driven by indignation against one's neighbor when it is not preceded by the consideration of Christian charity. It is an excessive outpouring of spiritual corruption, which, in a certain sense, could be called malice. This sin is particularly dangerous because it takes hold in the noblest part of mankind—the heart—making it exceedingly difficult to cast out once it has taken root. Would you like proof? You may find a man who appears peaceful, meek, and gentle, to the point that it seems impossible for wrath to dwell in him. Yet if you provoke him with something displeasing, you will soon see how the wrath that lay hidden within his soul comes forth. It is much like quicklime: as long as you do not pour water on it, it remains still, but as soon as water is added, it begins to boil. Similarly, if you pour a little Christian charity upon wrath, you will immediately extinguish it.

To prevent wrath from arising, you must be quick to listen but slow to speak. However, this is not enough; you must also train yourself to exercise self-restraint and master your emotions. The first step, as I have said, is to be slow to speak when you are angered. The second, which is even more perfect, is to resolve in your heart never to allow yourself to be angered, no matter what provocation arises. Indeed, you may even test yourself at times to see if you are strong enough to endure an offense without reacting in anger against the one who wronged you. Sacred Scripture speaks extensively about wrath, particularly in the writings of Saint James, who also provides remedies for it. There is, however, another type of wrath that is righteous and good. This occurs when we become angry not against a person, but against sin itself. Moreover, as the prophet David teaches, we must cultivate a form of wrath against our own vices and sins in order to avoid falling into iniquity.

**Eusebius:** You have spoken so aptly to my concerns, as if you knew my very intentions. I trust you will do the same with the fourth deadly sin, which is gluttony.

**Archbishop:** Saint Paul classifies this sin under the First Commandment when he states that "the god of the wicked is their belly." This applies to all who live as though their purpose is to eat, rather than eating in order to live, for in such persons the Apostle's saying is well fulfilled: their god is their stomach. We may also rightly say that this sin is prohibited by the Sixth Commandment, for in commanding us to be chaste, it necessarily commands us to adopt the means of maintaining chastity—namely, temperance in food, limited sleep, physical labor, prayer, reading, contemplation, study, performing good works for one's neighbor, and enduring hardships such as cold, heat, and poverty.

**Eusebius:** By my salvation, this explanation pleases me greatly, for in few words you have said much.

**Antronio:** Indeed, you have; though I would have wished for a more detailed exposition. But since you consider it sufficient, let us proceed to the fifth deadly sin, which is envy.

**Archbishop:** I tell you in all sincerity that I regard this sin as the gravest of all, for it seems to stem from a base and petty spirit. The one who commits this sin transgresses against all ten commandments, for he directly opposes the virtue of charity upon which they are all founded. Yet from the words of Saint John, we see clearly that the commandment most directly violated by this sin is the Fifth, for he states that "whoever hates his brother," harboring envy against him, "is a murderer." For this reason, I find it most fitting what I once read in Saint Augustine—that we must resist anger so that it does not turn into envy and enmity. He seems to have understood that anger is like a sapling, while envy is like a great tree. Therefore, he commands that we cut down the sapling of anger before it grows into the great tree of envy.

**Eusebius:** That is well said. Now remains the final deadly sin—sloth.

**Archbishop:** This is the last snare by which the devil seeks to entangle the soul. It is prohibited in the Third Commandment, which commands us to sanctify the Sabbath. We offend God in this sin in two ways: bodily and spiritually. We sin bodily when we neglect to attend Mass and sermons, when we fail to pray, to read, and to engage in other exercises that are or can be holy and good. We sin spiritually when, having begun to walk the path of virtue—the path of God—we grow negligent, become complacent, and lose both the love and fear of God. Of such people, Scripture declares that they are accursed, for they perform the works of God negligently. From this sin arise hypocrites and false Christians. Moreover, I have often observed that the devil, under the guise of good, deceives even those who are otherwise outstanding in virtue, leading them miserably into this sin.

**Eusebius:** In what manner does he do this?

**Archbishop:** He convinces them that peace and tranquility are of great value—which, of course, they cannot deny. Then, under the pretext of not wanting to lose that which they already recognize as good, he leads them to neglect the good they could do for their neighbor. In this way, he causes them to bury the talent that God has given them, rather than using it to serve others.

**Eusebius:** Your reasoning seems entirely sound, and I have no doubt that this same principle is what led you to abandon your own quiet and repose—where you were engaged only with God and your books—to take upon yourself the burdensome office of this archbishopric.

**Archbishop:** God alone knows the truth of that, and may it please Him that I act in such a way that my works make it evident to all. But to conclude our discussion of this sin and of all the others, I say that the most effective and genuine remedy I have found—and the one that, in my opinion, you, as a parish priest, should especially commend to your children—is that every Christian should have a firm and unwavering will never to offend God under any circumstance. He must also recognize, along with this resolve, how dangerous and subtle the snares of the devil are, and how inclined the human soul is toward evil. He must understand that the very moment he believes himself most secure is often the moment of greatest peril. In short, he must always consider that in all these sins, whether great or small, he offends God. Moreover, with this awareness, he must utterly distrust his own natural strength, for it is undoubtedly insufficient for such a great endeavor. He must therefore earnestly seek God's help and favor, asking Him persistently for the grace to overcome all these vices in general and, in particular, the one that most afflicts him. At the same time, he must hold firm confidence that God will grant what he asks. Ultimately, it is of great benefit to abhor sin and love virtue, to imitate any good we see to the best of our ability, and to flee from evil as one would from deadly poison. Let me assure you, whoever possesses this disposition is close to goodness, while he who lacks it is already ensnared in evil. Thus, I say that true repentance belongs only to the one who genuinely detests his sin and forsakes it entirely.

**Antronio:** By the sacred orders I have received, I can say nothing but this: to do what you prescribe, I would need to be utterly broken down and remade anew. Oh, may God help us! What blindness we live in! What darkness surrounds us, even we who consider ourselves to be the light of the world and the salt of the earth! Out of charity, my lord, since our Lord has granted you such grace, do not weary of speaking with us. And now, tell me: why have you said nothing about the circumstances that aggravate sin? In our confessions, we place so much emphasis on them.

**Archbishop:** Listen carefully, Father. My purpose in all my discourses is to show you what is necessary for us all to be true Christians—genuine, not counterfeit; evangelical, not mere ceremonialists; spiritual, not superstitious; possessing noble souls, not scrupulous minds. I seek to instill in us a Christianity that is rooted in the sincerity of the soul, not merely in outward appearances. Above all, I want us to understand what true evangelical freedom consists of and how far it extends. Thus, we must recognize that if we are now as children in Christ—by which I mean that Christ has not yet been fully formed within our souls—then we must labor to nurture Him within us. And when shall we say that He is fully formed? When we have become mature and perfect men in Christ. To this perfection, every Christian is undoubtedly called—if not to fully attain it, then at the very least to strive for it earnestly. For this reason, I am thoroughly convinced that excessive scrutiny of circumstances, as some scrupulous individuals engage in, is harmful in some ways. It breeds unnecessary doubts in the conscience, and those who suffer from such scruples are like the weak-willed women whom Saint Paul reproves—always learning but never arriving at a full knowledge of the truth. Would you like to know what I find to be the principal factor that either aggravates or mitigates sin? It is the disposition of the heart with which the act is committed.

**Antronio:** I do not understand what you mean unless you explain it further.

**Archbishop:** You must understand that, among others, there are generally two kinds of men who fall into sin. Some sin out of weakness—these are those who, when tempted, cannot easily resist and thus succumb. Such was the case with David when he sinned with Bathsheba and contrived to have her husband killed. Such was also the case with Saint Peter when he denied Christ. And if you read *Vitas Patrum*, you will find many examples of individuals who, though they fell into sin due to weakness and the force of temptation—not out of malice or wicked intent—immediately repented upon realizing their sin and rose again. Then there are others who sin not because they are tempted but because they have developed a wicked habit of sinning and do so with deliberate malice. Just as they love vice, so too do they remain in it, unwilling to depart from it even if they so desired. In my view, such men sin because of their lack of faith. If they possessed faith, it would lead them to a true knowledge of God, and in knowing Him, I assure you, they would come to despise the very vices they once loved. Thus, we may say that just as the first group sins out of frailty and weakness, the latter sins out of infidelity. This is why you will see certain individuals so at ease and complacent in their sins, as if they expected to attain some form of blessedness through them. I will not speak now of what I think about the confessions of such men, as none of them are present here; but one day, I shall make them understand how lost they truly are and how the fruit of their perdition will be eternal punishment.

**Eusebius:** May God grant that you do as you have said, and may it be as beneficial as we all hope, for truly, this is a matter of great spiritual ruin. Now, I must tell you that your classification of sinners has helped me understand certain passages of Sacred Scripture that, without this distinction, seemed obscure to me.

**Archbishop:** I assure you, the one who first explained this to me also used it to clarify for me certain passages that I had never before understood, not even in thought.

**Eusebius:** Well then, share one with us.

**Archbishop:** This is not the time for it, so if you agree, let us leave it for another day.

**Eusebius:** You speak wisely. Let it be as you say, for the day is long, and there will be time for all things. Now, tell us specifically about the works of mercy, both corporal and spiritual.

**Archbishop:** Listen, brothers: for the Christian who truly loves God and his neighbor, it is evident that he is obliged to assist others in all their needs, in whatever way possible—just as he himself would wish to be helped in his own distress. In my opinion, there is little need to list these works of mercy; and, in truth, there is little need for others to do so as well, for no man is so devoid of reason as not to know that he is bound to do for his neighbor what he would wish to be done for himself.

**Eusebius:** Then tell me, why were these seven works specifically identified?

**Archbishop:** You should ask that of the one who designated them, for I neither know nor care to know.

**Eusebius:** By my salvation, you are right. But since you do not wish to speak on that, then tell us about the cardinal virtues. First, explain why they are given this name.

**Archbishop:** They are called by this name because, through them, we have inherited a term from the pagan philosophers, who named them cardinal virtues, believing that human life is governed and upheld by them, as a door turns on its hinges. However, among Christians, it would be fitting for these virtues to lose their name, for we possess others far greater, which we call theological virtues.

**Eusebius:** Then what would you have them called?

**Archbishop:** They could rightly be called moral virtues, since they serve to instruct a man in human conduct and can be possessed even by one who is not a Christian.

**Eusebius:** How so?

**Archbishop:** In this manner: Prudence, which consists in the proper knowledge of things, enables a person to speak with honesty and moderation in all circumstances, to engage in useful and upright affairs, and to treat each person as is fitting. Clearly, this is a moral virtue, and thus, even a pagan may possess it.

Likewise, justice, which consists in fairness, rendering to each his due, presents a strong semblance of virtue. A man who possesses it is rightly called upright, for justice is closely bound to goodness and clemency. It too is a moral virtue that may exist in one who is not a Christian.

Furthermore, magnanimity, the third virtue, which is also known as fortitude, consists in undertaking great and arduous deeds, in despising worldly things that are inferior to mankind, and in neither being overly distressed by adversity nor excessively elated by prosperity. This, too, is a moral virtue.

Finally, there is temperance, the fourth virtue, which consists in self-restraint, not only in illicit acts but also in all emotions and affections. It makes a man master of his desires rather than their servant and inclines him to modesty and endurance, so that he in no way deviates from what is honest and good. Like the others, this virtue is also moral.

You can see, then, that these virtues may exist in a man who, as I have said, is not a Christian.

Yet just as they might lead such a man to fall into the sin of pride—since, failing to attribute them to God and to direct them toward Him, he would inevitably become vain in possessing them—so too, if these virtues reside in a Christian soul, they contain great benefit. In order for them to be true virtues, however, we must make them Christian and baptize them. If we baptize them, there is no harm in removing the pagan name by which they are known—especially since we see that they unjustly claim it.

And when you, Father, instruct your children and others in these virtues, it would be well to apply them to the doctrine of Christ, so that when they later encounter them in the writings of some philosopher, they may understand them as Christians, not as mere philosophers.

**Antronio:** I will gladly do so, even if only because I am an enemy of these philosophies and profane letters. But you must tell me how I ought to proceed.

**Archbishop:** How now, Father? Have you spent any time studying these writings?

**Antronio:** No, in truth, nor would I have wished to.

**Archbishop:** Then why do you hold such a low opinion of what you do not know?

**Antronio:** By your life, do not draw me into such questions; just answer what I have asked you.

**Archbishop:** Very well, I shall do so. You must know that prudence is commended to us by Christ our Lord when He said: "Be wise as serpents and innocent as doves." Justice is likewise enjoined upon us when He commanded: "Do unto others as you would have them do unto you." Magnanimity is encouraged when, strengthening His disciples, He said: "Do not fear those who kill the body but cannot kill the soul." And temperance is taught in His words: "Whoever looks at a woman with lust has already committed adultery with her in his heart." This, then, is how you may apply these virtues to Christian teaching.

**Antronio:** That is well said; but for me to understand them fully and to grasp those scriptural references, it would be necessary for you to explain them in greater depth.

**Archbishop:** I will do so, but another day.

**Eusebius:** You speak wisely. And since you have spoken so nobly about these virtues, despite doing so reluctantly, I implore you, by your life, to now speak to us of the *theological* virtues, for since these are uniquely Christian, I know you will take great delight in discussing them.

**Archbishop:** That I shall indeed. And whereas in everything else I have said, you owe me your gratitude, for this I must instead thank you—for your willingness to listen. For whenever I speak of these virtues, I feel most clearly that they begin anew to grow within my soul in a fresh and greater measure. May it please God that they grow in yours likewise, for truly, the entire purpose of Christian discourse should be this.

Now, there are three theological virtues: faith, hope, and charity. These are so intimately joined together that one necessarily gives rise to the others. Thus, I hold it as certain that whoever possesses one of them perfectly will necessarily possess all three.

Let us begin, then, with the first—faith. First, you must understand that in Sacred Scripture, the word faith is taken in two different senses. In one sense, faith is understood as a certainty and belief in things unseen. This kind of faith may be dead, without works, and can be found even in a thief or a murderer, albeit in an imperfect form. You must know that Sacred Scripture speaks but rarely of this kind of faith, and it is this faith that Saint James says is dead when it is not accompanied by charity—meaning that it is of little worth.

In the second sense, faith is understood as trust—as when we hear the words of God, and after believing them to be His and true, we place all our confidence in Him to fulfill them. This is living faith, which is the root of works of charity. Just as the branches grow from the root of a tree, and where there is a root, branches must necessarily sprout in due time, so too, where this kind of faith exists, works of charity inevitably follow, for faith cannot be preserved without them. I will say even more: this faith, which theologians call formed faith, is like a living fire in the hearts of the faithful, by which they are daily purified and drawn closer to God. That is why I compare it to fire—just as it is impossible for fire not to produce heat, so too it is impossible for true faith not to produce works of charity. If it does not, it ceases to be true faith. From all this, we may rightly conclude that for a Christian to have faith, he must both believe in God and believe God.

**Antronio:** I need a clearer explanation of that.

**Archbishop:** I will explain it to you. When I say that one must *believe God*, I mean that he must believe everything written in Sacred Scripture concerning Him. When I say that one must *believe in God*, I mean that he must trust entirely in God as his ultimate end and rely on His promises—even when they seem beyond human reason. In such cases, reason itself must be brought into submission under the obedience of faith.

**Eusebius:** Tell me, then—does this not confuse faith with hope?

**Archbishop:** Not at all. And to make this distinction clearer, I will give you a comparison; and in doing so, we will also have explained what hope is.

Imagine a man whose head and feet are made of wax, standing on one side of a mountain that is entirely ablaze with fire. Another man comes to him and says: "If you wish to cross to the other side, where there is a most delightful place, put your trust in me and take my hand. I will lead you through the fire, and as long as you do not let go of me for any reason, I will bring you safely to the place I have promised."

Now, though this seems impossible, the man, trusting in his guide, steps into the fire. Even when he stumbles and falls along the way, he never loses confidence in the one leading him. Instead, he rises again and continues forward—this is faith. At the same time, this man also has great hope that his guide, once they have passed through the mountain, will bring him to the delightful place he promised, as long as he does not abandon him—this is hope.

**Eusebius:** By my salvation, that is a most excellent comparison!

**Antronio:** For the love of God, I beg you to explain it further so that I may understand it better, for it seems to contain great moral teaching.

**Eusebius:** Indeed, it does—perhaps even more than you think. But let us not delay now; remind me later when we have more time, and I will explain it to you at length.

**Archbishop:** He speaks wisely. Now that we have spoken of faith and hope, it remains for us to discuss charity.

Of the things I previously mentioned regarding this mother and root of all virtues—charity—when speaking on the Creed and the two commandments of the love of God and neighbor, I trust you still remember them. Therefore, I refer you back to those teachings, for charity is nothing other than love for God and for our neighbor. It is absolutely necessary that this virtue be deeply embedded in our hearts, for without it, we cannot be Christians. This is the mark that Christ our Lord willed for His followers, distinguishing them from all others: "By this, all men will know that you are my disciples: if you love one another." Christ also gave us a new commandment concerning this charity when He said: "A new commandment I give you: that you love one another as I have loved you." This is the virtue of which Saint Paul speaks so often in his epistles, exalting it above all others. Saint Peter tells us that it is charity that covers a multitude of sins. Saint Paul even places it above faith and hope, declaring that without it, all else is worthless, even if one possessed all other virtues. And finally, he states that charity never fails—it does not end, even when this life ends. If I were to tell you everything that I have gathered from Sacred Scripture concerning this virtue, I would never finish. But to conclude, I say this: if you reflect carefully, you will see that the bond between faith, hope, and charity is so strong that one cannot exist without the others. For whoever has true and living faith also has charity, for in believing, he comes to know, and in knowing, he comes to love; and in loving, he acts. Likewise, he who knows, believes, and loves also hopes in the One he has come to know, believe, and love.

**Eusebius:** Your words have captivated me! Blessed be God, who has given you such wisdom and insight. May His infinite goodness and mercy cause these words to bear fruit in our souls, just as you said at the beginning. Oh, if only there were a time when these truths were preached from the pulpits in this manner, for it is of the utmost importance that every Christian know them!

**Archbishop:** Indeed, and because I see that they are not often preached, I am determined to ensure that each father instructs his son in these teachings, and that every teacher imparts them to his disciple.

**Antronio:** And what if the father does not know them?

**Archbishop:** Then he must seek to learn them; and if he refuses to do so, wishing only to be ignorant himself, let him at least find someone who can teach his son— for such knowledge will be of greater worth to the child than any inheritance his father could leave him.

**Antronio:** Oh yes, you won't have to look far—every corner is filled with those who know and are willing to teach these things!

**Eusebius:** Let us put aside such objections, for I assure you, if people sought them out, they would find them. But—alas!—a wicked father does not care whether his son becomes as corrupt as himself. Yet let us leave this aside, for it is a waste of time. If our questions do not weary you, tell us now what we should teach concerning the gifts of the Holy Spirit.

**Archbishop:** That I shall gladly do! And I want you to know something about me: day and night, I never grow weary of speaking about the things we discuss here, for I find my rest in meditating upon and speaking of Christian truths. Since you wish to hear about the gifts of the Holy Spirit, listen carefully and pay close attention.

**Antronio:** That pleases us.

**Archbishop:** Of the gifts that God bestows upon the soul He chooses for Himself, which we rightly call the gifts of the Holy Spirit, I would wish to speak at great length, sharing all that I know and feel, and all that I wish others to know and feel. But it is better that I give you a brief outline of each, so that you may, in turn, teach your people what you judge most necessary for them. May it please the goodness of God that, in speaking of them, they become so deeply impressed upon our souls that they remain there forever. You should know that these gifts are spoken of primarily by the prophet Isaiah in the passage that begins: "A shoot will come up from the stump of Jesse, and a branch will bear fruit from his roots." In this passage, he lists seven gifts with which the soul of Christ, our Lord and Redeemer, was endowed. And although these gifts were all present in Him in perfect fullness, God distributes them among us according to our capacity. Saint Paul speaks at length about this distribution of gifts in one of his epistles, where he describes the different offices that God appoints within His Church. You would do well to read this, which you will find in the twelfth chapter of the First Epistle to the Corinthians.

**Eusebius:** Having established this, let us now discuss how each of these gifts is to be understood, what we should believe about them, and what effect each has on the soul of the Christian.

**Archbishop:** First, the gift of wisdom is given by God to the soul so that it may know and delight in Him. More particularly, He grants it to those who are called to teach others, so that through this gift, they may instruct in all truth with great fervor and without fear—not for personal gain or out of ambition to be esteemed as wise, but solely to magnify and exalt the doctrine of Christ and to imprint it deeply upon the souls of all. This is the wisdom with which the Apostles spoke, and through it, they tasted and felt the truths they proclaimed. It is to this wisdom that the words of Solomon in the Song of Songs refer: "At the fragrance of your perfume, the maidens run after you." This is the wisdom with which the holy Scholars of the

Church wrote. Thus, you must understand this gift as divine wisdom, and this is the effect it produces in the soul: for as wisdom from heaven is a most delightful knowledge, it impresses itself so deeply within our spirits that it fills us with fervor and power to proclaim the goodness and mercy of God in a manner utterly different from what we could achieve through mere human learning. Even if we possessed all the knowledge attainable by natural means, it would not compare to the wisdom infused by the Spirit of God.

The second gift, understanding, is given by God to those who must hear doctrine, so that through it, they may listen attentively, comprehend with love, and, having understood, apply what they have learned according to their needs and make full use of it. Thus, the soul that receives this high gift knows well how to apply all things to itself and to derive benefit from everything. In all things, it perceives God; everything speaks to it of His greatness, goodness, omnipotence, and wisdom. It sees Him in all, finds Him in all, and understands all in a way that leads to salvation. In short, wisdom arms the mouth, while understanding arms the heart.

The third gift, counsel, is given by God to the soul so that it may know how to give sound advice to others and even to apply it to itself. This is the gift that enables the righteous to provide good and holy counsel to those who seek it.

**Antronio:** To me, this gift seems to be the same as the first.

**Archbishop:** Why so?

**Antronio:** Because I believe that whoever possesses wisdom must also possess counsel.

**Archbishop:** You are mistaken. Many times, a person may have wisdom but lack counsel. Would you like to see proof of this from Sacred Scripture? Do you not believe that Moses had the gift of wisdom?

**Antronio:** Yes, without any doubt, and in great measure.

**Archbishop:** Then consider how he lacked the gift of counsel. As it is recounted in Exodus, Moses was burdened with the great task of serving as the sole judge for all the disputes among the people of Israel. When his father-in-law, Jethro, came to see him, he advised Moses to delegate this responsibility to twelve chosen men from among the people, for otherwise, he would not be able to bear it. Moses found his father-in-law's counsel wise and put it into practice. Here, then, you see how what Moses lacked, Jethro possessed—namely, the gift of counsel. Perhaps one could even bring into this discussion the instance when Saint Paul rebuked Saint Peter.

**Eusebius:** No need to say more; that example is sufficient. You have well proven your point, so let us proceed.

**Archbishop:** You speak rightly.

The fourth gift, fortitude, is given by God to the one who has received counsel so that he may act upon it with courage, strength, and perseverance. This gift is necessary for all, for we all require counsel—some more, some less—but no one is exempt, no matter how self-reliant he may seem. And often, the one who believes he needs it the least is actually the one in greatest need of it.

**Eusebius:** Truly, you speak a great truth. I know some individuals who, though good and wise in certain respects, have fallen into difficulties simply because they placed too much confidence in their own judgment and refused to accept the advice given to them in charity and holy zeal. And yet, they could have easily avoided such troubles at little cost.

**Archbishop:** You have spoken precisely to my point, and I would like to discuss this matter further with you, but let us leave it for another day. Now, let us move forward.

The fifth gift, knowledge (science), is given by God to those whom He chooses as preachers and heralds of His sacred doctrine.

**Antronio:** Let us see—what difference do you make between wisdom and knowledge? To me, they seem to be the same thing.

**Archbishop:** I will explain it to you. Wisdom, which is savory knowledge, is given to know, taste, and experience God. The more of this wisdom the soul possesses, the more it knows, experiences, and delights in Him. God often grants this wisdom to an old woman or an unlearned man while withholding it from a great scholar. So much so that if you speak to such a learned man about it, he might find it incomprehensible or think it nonsense. Knowledge, on the other hand, is given particularly to those who are to teach the Word of God. This is the gift that Christ promised to His apostles, telling them that no man would be able to resist it. It is true that these two terms—wisdom and knowledge—are sometimes used interchangeably, with wisdom being taken for knowledge and vice versa. However, be careful not to confuse this divine knowledge with the kind acquired through human effort alone, for such knowledge merely puffs up and fosters pride.

**Antronio:** Now I understand this well. Continue.

**Archbishop:** The sixth gift, piety, is given by God to sanctify the soul after it has received doctrine, for piety means holiness. Thus, whoever receives the gift of piety receives the gift of true religion and sanctity.

**Antronio:** Then, according to this, all Christians who have received the doctrine of Christ should be holy?

**Archbishop:** Indeed, that is what we ought to be. And if not all are, it is because the wicked fail in this duty, whereas the righteous fulfill it. For with the doctrine of the Gospel comes the gift of holiness, and all who embrace and practice it as they should are truly saints. It is for this reason that Saint Paul calls Christians saints.

**Antronio:** I do not believe it.

**Archbishop:** I do, for I know it well.

**Antronio:** Who told you?

**Archbishop:** I have read it many times in many places. Specifically, you will find it where Saint Paul, in sending greetings in his letters, writes: "All the saints greet you, especially those who are of Caesar's household."

**Antronio:** Say no more—I believe it. You have spoken nothing but the truth. Proceed.

**Archbishop:** The seventh gift, fear of the Lord, is given by God to keep the soul in a constant state of reverence and vigilance, lest it offend Him. This holy fear is an essential part of true religion, and it is exceedingly precious, for by it all the other gifts are preserved. The more the soul possesses this fear, the more carefully and faithfully it remains in God's grace and love.

This fear is entirely different from the fear that Saint John speaks of when he says that perfect love casts out fear, for he refers to a servile fear that is incompatible with true charity. The fear of the Lord, however, is the fear that David speaks of: "Come, my children, listen to me, and I will teach you the fear of the Lord." Scripture frequently praises this holy fear, as in these passages:

"He who fears the Lord will do good works."

"My son, when you come to serve the Lord, stand in righteousness and fear, and prepare your soul for temptation."

And in many other places, you will find this holy fear exalted.

So here, you have what I know concerning the gifts of the Holy Spirit. But beyond this, I know something even more profitable: that it is far better to experience and feel these gifts within the soul than merely to speak about them with the tongue. Oh, may God be my help! How great must be the sweetness and the wondrous joy that the soul feels when it perceives within itself these most precious jewels—or even a portion of them—bestowed upon it by the hand of its Bridegroom, Jesus Christ! What delight, what contentment, what peace! How rich and blessed it will find itself, possessing such true wealth! And how utterly it will count as refuse all those things that the lovers of this world consider to be riches! With what lordship it will hold them! With what generosity it will distribute them! I hold it as most certain that only the one who delights in these spiritual riches can properly despise material wealth and master it rather than be mastered by it. When I reflect on this, I think little of the sufferings, trials, torments, humiliations, and martyrdoms that the holy martyrs endured. For without a doubt, their souls were adorned with these rich jewels, which they recognized as a kind of pledge or foretaste of eternal life. Moreover, they were led to martyrdom by love—the love which, as the wise man says, is as strong as death.

**Eusebius:** By my faith, your words have such power that I believe they would be enough to stir even the hardest heart—especially when you speak with such fervor!

**Antronio:** Do you know what I have noticed? You have never yet asked him about the commandments of the Church. And to tell you the truth, this is what I most desire to know.

**Eusebius:** Do not think that I have forgotten them! But since what I have asked so far is more essential, I have set them aside for now.

**Antronio:** How is it more essential?

**Eusebius:** I will explain. It is more necessary for a Christian to know what he must do before God than what he must do before the Church. For we are not bound to serve God because of the Church, but rather, we serve the Church because of God.

**Antronio:** I must say, you are right. But still, if you permit it, I would like us to hear something about these commandments.

**Archbishop:** I will speak on them, to please you.

First of all, you already know that the commandments commonly referred to as the commandments of the Church are five. We will discuss each one in order, explaining what we believe every Christian should know about them—especially what you should teach to those under your care, for that is our principal purpose.

The first commandment is to hear the entire Mass every Sunday and on holy days of obligation. The Church's reasoning behind this commandment is that, having decreed that on such days we should abstain from physical labor—so that in honor of these feasts we might dedicate ourselves to spiritual matters—it deemed it necessary to require our presence in church, where we might wholly and entirely offer ourselves to God. Furthermore, on these days, we are to listen to sermons that might edify our souls with sound and sacred doctrine.

The Church commands us to hear Mass so that we may comprehend the mysteries represented therein and likewise benefit from the doctrine read to us in the Epistle and the Holy Gospel. Considering this, one must not assume that those who do not engage their minds in the words spoken during the Mass have fulfilled the Church's mandate. On the contrary, those who spend the entire time conversing about matters unworthy even of their own hearths fail in their duty. Likewise, those who bring their prayer books and rosaries to church, only to recite prayers throughout the Mass, counting the number of Psalms and *Paternosters* they have completed as if their piety increased in proportion, also err. They believe they have rendered a greater service to God, yet, in truth, I would not dare assess the worth of such prayers, for I observe that if, upon leaving the church, they were asked which Gospel was sung at Mass or what was stated in the Epistle, they would be entirely unable to answer, no more than if they had been in the Indies.

**Antronio:** And do you say that such individuals fail to fulfill the Church's intent?

**Archbishop:** Indeed, without question. Furthermore, I say this: it would have been better for the first group to remain at home and for the second to close their prayer books, at least during the reading of the Epistle, the Gospel, and the public prayers of the Mass.

**Antronio:** That is reasonable; I understand you now. Tell me, then, how you believe one should instruct others in properly hearing Mass.

**Archbishop:** First and foremost, you should instruct them, if possible, to familiarize themselves beforehand with the Gospel and Epistle that will be read on that day. Upon entering the church, they should position themselves in a place where they will not be disturbed by idle chatter, which might rob them of the peace and attentiveness they ought to maintain. They should hear the Mass with great devotion and attention, carefully noting all that is done, represented, and proclaimed therein. Above all, they should pay close attention to the Gospel and the Epistle so that they may reflect on them throughout the day and engage in meaningful discussion regarding what they have heard.

**Antronio:** Do you hold the Epistle and the Gospel in such little regard that you wish even children and women to discuss them?

**Archbishop:** What a peculiar thought! Quite the opposite, because I hold them in the highest regard and deem them essential, I desire that all should discuss them.

**Antronio:** You astonish me with such a novel and seemingly unreasonable notion.

**Eusebius:** By my life, I cannot tolerate such a notion. Tell me, for your own sake, would you consider it wrong for a young boy to know what His Lordship has taught us here?

**Antronio:** Certainly not. I am not so irrational as to disapprove of what is good.

**Eusebius:** And how do you believe he might learn it?

**Antronio:** By being taught and discussing it.

**Eusebius:** Then you see that you should consider it entirely good for all to do the same. Would you not approve of one who had done so?

**Antronio:** I concede that you are right, but you must understand that I am not inventing these objections of my own accord.

**Eusebius:** That I do believe; yet I also believe that if you had not allowed such a corrupt and un-Christian opinion to take root in your mind, you would not now be attempting to cast it out. From now on, take this truth as firmly established: we are as we converse and as the books we habitually read shape us. Therefore, if you desire your subjects to be holy and virtuous, you should encourage them to read and speak of holy and virtuous matters. The holier the subject, the better it is. And since the holiest teachings are those of Jesus Christ, Our Lord, and His apostles, you must counsel your subjects to engage in them continuously.

**Antronio:** Very well, I shall do as you command. Continue instructing us.

**Archbishop:** Likewise, tell them that whenever there is a sermon, they should listen to it with great attention. If the preacher speaks wisely, delivering Christian and evangelical teachings, they should receive them with eagerness and ask God to imprint them upon their souls. But if the preacher is foolish or frivolous, they should still listen, so that, stirred by Christian zeal, they may grieve over the dishonor done to God and His most sacred doctrine, and fervently pray that He may send good and holy laborers into His vineyard, which is the Church. This, in my judgment, is what you should instruct them concerning this commandment. And if you see fit, you should also make them understand that those who do not observe it in this manner fail to fulfill the Church's intention.

**Antronio:** I promise to do everything exactly as you have said. Now that this matter is settled, tell me about the second commandment.

**Archbishop:** The second commandment is that we must confess at least once a year during Lent. I could say much about confession, for I have studied it with great diligence, but we may discuss it at length another time. For now, I shall only say what is necessary for the parish priest to instruct his subjects. First, you must tell them that confession was instituted as a remedy for sin. That is, if after receiving the Most Holy Water of Baptism we should sin, we may, by recognizing our sin and confessing it, obtain God's forgiveness. Having explained this, tell them what a great blessing it is to have no need of confession throughout one's life.

**Antronio:** What! And do you consider that to be good?

**Archbishop:** Not only good but exceedingly good.

**Antronio:** Why?

**Archbishop:** Because if it is good that one does not sin, then it must also be good that one has no need to confess.

**Antronio:** That is impossible.

**Archbishop:** Do not say that, for your own sake, for it is a grave error. Do you not believe that with the grace of God, it is possible?

**Antronio:** Yes, but…

**Archbishop:** Do not say "but," for if it is possible through the grace of God, and it is possible to obtain the grace of God, then it is also possible to avoid committing mortal sin. And if one does not commit mortal sin, then there would be no need for confession.

**Antronio:** I concede that you are right, but do you not see that, in this way, one would not fulfill this commandment of the Church if they were never to confess throughout their life?

**Archbishop:** You misunderstood me. I said that they would not confess out of necessity in their lifetime. What I meant was that it is good for them to confess even when there is no necessity, whenever the Church commands it. There are many reasons for this, which would take too long to explain.

**Antronio:** I am quite satisfied with your reasoning. But, for your own sake, tell me—why is it that those whom we commonly see as the best Christians, those who live most virtuously and piously, confess more frequently?

**Archbishop:** Would that God had granted me full understanding of this matter, for I would gladly explain it.

**Antronio:** Still, I wish to hear your thoughts on it.

**Archbishop:** What I can tell you is that I would desire never to do anything that would require confession, nor anything that would trouble my conscience. Thus, I would confess only once a year, solely to fulfill the commandment of the Church. As for those whom you call the best Christians, I do not believe my judgment is sufficient to assess them. However, I have no doubt that if such people knew what should truly be understood about confession—what a Christian is obligated to confess and what he is not—perhaps, if they are indeed as you describe them, they would confess less frequently. Unless, of course, they believe there is some inherent sanctity in frequent confession, in which case, I say nothing.

**Antronio:** Then, for charity's sake, tell us—what is it that we must confess?

**Archbishop:** You ask much of me, but in short, I tell you this: one must confess only those things for which one's conscience accuses them—those offenses committed against God, whether through ignorance, weakness, or malice.

**Eusebius:** I must say that your words have satisfied me more than you might think, for I give you my word that many times

I have gone to confession, and, simply to have something to say, I have confessed things for which my conscience does not accuse me in the slightest. I have also noticed the same tendency in some who come to confess alongside me. In truth, while this is not necessarily evil, it is not good either—it is, in fact, closer to error than to virtue.

**Antronio:** Since you have made your confession, it is only fitting that I make mine. I must tell you that, by the ordination I have received, I never approach confession with any such reflection. I neither examine whether my conscience accuses me nor whether it does not. Rather, I confess merely out of habit, believing that if I were to omit it, I would be lost. Indeed, I promise you that I believe most clerics do the same. This must be evident to those who hear our confessions, for the very same sins we confessed in times past we confess again today, just as we did yesterday.

**Archbishop:** Let us not dwell further on such confessions, for I could also say much on the matter—recounting what my companions, when we were but boys, would tell me after they returned from confession regarding the manner in which their confessors dealt with them. For my part, I do not know why some confessors act as they do, nor what they truly think of confession—whether they regard it as instituted for the healing of souls or for their own gain. But it is better to remain silent, for nothing would be gained from discussing it.

Returning to what I previously said, you must instruct all that, should they fall into sin out of weakness, they should ask God's forgiveness and then make use of confession as a remedy. This must be done with great prudence and discretion, not confessing more than what their conscience truly accuses them of, and doing so briefly, without engaging in idle or excessive discourse. You must also warn them that the only motive for confession should be sincere sorrow for having offended God. This applies to those who come to confess.

Beyond this, confessors must be careful not to lead penitents into sin. I say this because it has become common practice for many to inquire into matters during confession that would be better left unsaid. Indeed, I must confess that I have learned of various sins from foolish confessors—sins I had never known before. It would be sufficient, after hearing the penitent's confession, for the confessor simply to absolve them, offering guidance and admonition as appropriate regarding what they have confessed. In doing so, he should encourage them not only to guard against sinning in the future but also to believe firmly that God has already forgiven their sins through their confession and the priest's absolution.

If confession were carried out in this manner, the conscience of the penitent would be at peace, and many frivolous—indeed, I might say disgraceful—practices that occur under the guise of confession would be avoided. The penance assigned to the one confessing should primarily include directing them to read a book containing sound doctrine and guidance suited to the sin to which they are most inclined, so that they may be better led away from it.

**Antronio:** I can only say that you are absolutely right in everything you have said. And since you explain everything so well, tell us now about the third commandment, which is to receive the Most Holy Sacrament at Easter.

**Archbishop:** You already know how this Most Holy Sacrament was instituted—on Holy Thursday, as Jesus Christ supped with His beloved apostles. He gave it to them after washing their feet, thereby teaching us that, in order to receive so great a guest into the dwelling of our souls, we must cleanse them of every stain of sin. Saint Paul teaches us the same in one of his epistles, and not without profound significance. Thus, I believe—and would that all believed it—that one of the effects of this Most Holy Sacrament is that it wonderfully aids the soul that receives it purely, enabling it to overcome entirely its inclination to sin. Moreover, I believe that one of the reasons why, in former times, Christians were accustomed to receive it daily was precisely because of this effect. Later, as the fervor of faith cooled and the fire of charity was extinguished, they began to receive it only on Sundays. Now, we have become so negligent that we have delayed it to once a year. For this reason, I insist that clerics and friars take great care in instructing the people on the proper understanding of this most exalted Sacrament, so that they may recognize that by receiving it worthily, they receive an increase of grace.

**Antronio:** Then, according to what you say was the ancient practice, is it indeed good to receive this Holy Sacrament frequently?

**Archbishop:** Who would say otherwise?

**Antronio:** Tell me, in order to receive it, is it necessary for a man to confess?

**Archbishop:** Yes, if he has something to confess. If he does not, then he need not confess, except when the Church commands it. Tell me, when you are to say Mass, do you confess if you have nothing to confess?

**Antronio:** No, for what purpose?

**Archbishop:** Then neither does one need to confess before receiving the Sacrament if he has nothing to confess.

**Antronio:** I concede that you are right. But if you saw someone going to receive Communion without first having confessed, would you not consider it a serious matter?

**Archbishop:** Certainly not, for I would assume of him what I would assume of myself—that he would confess if he had something to confess.

**Antronio:** I assure you that you will find very few who would say what you have just said in this matter.

**Archbishop:** You are mistaken, for I will find many who think as I do, though I also know that there will be more who say the contrary. The reason is that everywhere there are more foolish and ignorant men than good and discerning ones.

**Antronio:** In that, you are quite right. But tell me—do you think I should instruct young boys to receive Communion?

**Archbishop:** Yes, those who have discretion and have reached the proper age. And take care that you earnestly cultivate in them a deep love and devotion for this Most Holy Sacrament. Let them be so drawn to it that those who are not yet old enough to receive it may long for the day when they will, and those who are of age may fully recognize the immense blessing they receive in partaking of it.

**Antronio:** That I shall do most willingly, to the best of my ability. And since you have already spoken sufficiently on this matter, tell us now what should be taught regarding the fourth commandment.

**Archbishop:** I am willing, though I leave much unsaid concerning confession and the Most Holy Sacrament—but that can be discussed another day.

The fourth commandment is to fast on the days prescribed by the Church. We must understand the origins of fasting, its virtue, and the reasons that moved the Church to establish it as a precept—since it might seem that fasting ought to be voluntary. Finally, to ensure that our fasting is good, we must consider what conditions it must meet. Once we have discussed these points, you will see what is necessary to teach.

First, fasting began long before the coming of Jesus Christ, Our Lord. The first mention of it in Sacred Scripture is found in the Book of Numbers. However, at that time, fasting appeared to be a practice of bodily affliction, accompanied by silence and mourning. Later, the fasts observed by the holy fathers in the Egyptian desert took the form of continuous abstinence from all exquisite foods. They ate only what could be obtained with minimal effort in the land where they dwelled.

It made no difference to them whether it was meat or fish; they ate temperately, not to satisfy their bodies but merely to sustain their lives. This is the form of fasting that is praised throughout Sacred Scripture. This is the fasting I wish those who pride themselves on fasting would learn to practice—not merely abstaining from meat while spending twice as much on fish brought from unknown lands, thinking that as long as they do not eat meat, they may indulge until they burst. Such fasting, I do not consider fasting at all, nor do I regard it as anything but a vice.

True fasting, on the other hand, subjugates the desires of the flesh to the dominion of reason and brings the body into submission to the spirit. It draws the soul closer to God and fosters a hatred of carnal pleasures and excessive indulgence in food and drink.

Leaving this aside for now, over time, the Church, motivated by holy and good reasons, instituted the fasts we now observe, in the manner in which we observe them. It is true that superstitious individuals have corrupted this practice, as they have many other things, using it not according to the Church's intent but according to their own imaginings. But setting them aside—for they shall give account to God for what they do—I say that in this matter of fasting, I would not have you teach anything else, especially to children, except that the principal fast of a Christian must be abstinence from sin and vice. This is what you must most earnestly counsel them. As for the bodily fast, do not trouble yourself with instructing children in it. Rather, tell them plainly that while they are still young, they are not bound to fast.

**Antronio:** Why not? Is it not better that they fast, even if they are not obligated to do so?

**Archbishop:** No.

**Antronio:** Why not?

**Archbishop:** Because fasting often causes illness in young boys. The reason is that, knowing they will not eat supper, they overeat at midday, which often harms them. There is also another, greater problem that I see: if from childhood they are taught that great piety consists in excessive fasting, they will place their sense of holiness in that practice, and instead of making them truly pious and holy, you will make them superstitious and corrupt.

**Antronio:** And you seriously want me to tell the boys this?

**Archbishop:** Yes, and I mean it with all my heart.

**Antronio:** Well, I promise to follow your advice. However, in my judgment, it would still be good for them to fast, if only for the sake of forming good habits.

**Archbishop:** Ensure that their good habit is in loving God and their neighbor, and do not concern yourself with the rest.

**Antronio:** That pleases me. But now, tell me—what do you say about the payment of tithes and firstfruits, which is the fifth commandment of the Church?

**Archbishop:** What do you want me to say? Nothing.

**Antronio:** How so?

**Archbishop:** I will tell you. Since we are speaking openly, I will be honest: I consider the clergy to be so diligent in ensuring the payment of tithes that our parishioners' souls will not be burdened with unpaid dues when they depart for the next world. If only we were as diligent in instructing the people in Christian doctrine as we are in making sure they pay tithes and firstfruits! If this were the case, I assure you, we would all be saints.

**Antronio:** But do you not think it is right for the clergy to collect their revenues?

**Archbishop:** I do not say they should not be collected. But I say that it would be right for us to use them as we are obligated to, rather than as we do. Since the laity give us their earnings in exchange for Christian teaching, we should be sure to provide it.

We all know that Saint Paul was greater than any of us and had far better grounds to demand tithes—and even double tithes. Yet you also know that he was so modest that, to avoid burdening anyone or giving the impression that he preached Christ for profit, he never ceased from working day and night at his trade, earning with his own hands not only for himself but also for those who traveled with him. In many places, he speaks of this with just cause, and he instructs us to beware of those who, idly wandering about, seek to live off the labor of others. Considering this, I do not say it is wrong for us to collect our revenues, but I do say that it is right and just that those who provide for us receive from us that which they have a right to—namely, Christian teaching. If they do not receive this from us, then, believe me, we do not deserve the revenues we collect. Moreover, we are not only bound to provide them with doctrine in return for their tithes, but we are also obligated to spend these revenues on the purposes for which the Church intends them to be used. Frankly, I do not understand how we, as clergy, do not feel ashamed to spend on worldly and even profane pursuits the funds that have been given to us for the care of the poor.

**Antronio:** As for me, God will demand nothing of me regarding this matter.

**Archbishop:** How can you say that?

**Antronio:** At the very least, I do not spend my income, as those you mentioned do, on gambling, debauchery, or similar vices.

**Archbishop:** Then on what do you spend it?

**Antronio:** On maintaining my own honor and that of my relatives, as befits a person of my income and status.

**Archbishop:** And are you completely content with that?

**Antronio:** Yes, without a doubt. Why should I not be?

**Archbishop:** Because the income you receive was not given to you to uphold your honor or that of your relatives, but to uphold the honor of God and His Church. Therefore, you should not be too content with how you are using it.

**Antronio:** And how is the honor of God upheld?

**Archbishop:** By doing in all things what He wills, for God is honored by nothing more than the obedience of His creatures. This is what you, I, and everyone else should regard above all, and according to this principle, we should spend everything we have.

**Antronio:** That is well said. But what about the honor of the Church—what does it consist in?

**Archbishop:** In our obedience to her in all things. And since she commands us to use our resources for the aid of the poor and the needy, we must do so in order to uphold her honor. Do you not think that God and His Church would be greatly glorified if Christians had such love and charity for one another that those who have means would not allow the poor to suffer in need?

**Antronio:** Yes, certainly. But I do not understand why God would be displeased with me for spending my income as I have said.

**Archbishop:** If you do not understand it, I will explain it to you. Consider this, by your life: If you sent a servant to the marketplace in Medina del Campo with one hundred thousand maravedís, instructing him to spend some on his personal necessities and the rest on purchasing certain goods for your purposes, would you not expect him to carry out your wishes?

**Antronio:** Yes, without a doubt.

**Archbishop:** And if, instead of fulfilling your will, he spent the money on whatever pleased him, even if it were on good things, what would you do?

**Antronio:** I would make him repay me and, beyond that, I would punish him as I saw fit.

**Archbishop:** You have answered well and precisely to my point. Now, since you have answered so wisely, tell me: Did God not send you into the marketplace of this world?

**Antronio:** Yes, He did.

**Archbishop:** And did He not give you one hundred thousand maravedís—or more—in income, so that you might use it for what you need and for what He commands?

**Antronio:** He did.

**Archbishop:** And if you, instead of using your income for what God wills, spend it on maintaining your own honor and that of your relatives, do you not think that He will have just cause to punish you, just as you said you would punish your own servant?

**Antronio:** It seems so. But since God grants me permission to take what I need for myself—and I consider my own honor and that of my relatives to be of great necessity—it is surely lawful for me to spend my income on this.

**Archbishop:** Let us see—what do you mean by honor?

**Antronio:** To live in the same status and authority as other persons who hold the same rank and income as I do.

**Archbishop:** Listen carefully, Father—you are gravely mistaken in this. It is lawful for you to take from your income only what is necessary for your station in life, and even that, moderately, without regard for what dignity or revenue you hold. For the honor of your office consists in fulfilling its duties, not in having fine horses and many servants. The honor of a Christian should consist in avoiding anything that is shameful before God and men, not in any worldly vanity. The honor you claim to uphold is the path to hell, for it is inseparably bound to greed and ambition. And so that you may better understand what I mean, let me tell you something about the first Archbishop of this Church, with whom I lived for many years. His name was Don Fray Fernando de Talavera, whose doctrine and holiness, I am sure, you have heard of.

**Antronio:** Yes, I have heard of him many times.

**Archbishop:** You must know that he had unmarried sisters who, had he not been Archbishop, would have married common tradesmen. However, since their brother had attained a high ecclesiastical position, they raised their expectations and asked him to arrange their marriages with noblemen, believing this would be fitting for his dignity. But the good man, understanding that the revenues of the Church were not meant to sustain worldly honors, refused to do so. Instead, he told them that if they wished to marry, he would give each of them thirty thousand maravedís, as he would to any orphan, with which they could marry tradesmen of their choosing. However, if they desired anything more, they would have to excuse him, for he could not, in good conscience, provide it. Do you think this holy man was concerned with maintaining his own honor or that of his family with the Church's wealth?

**Antronio:** No, certainly not. But do you not see that this was an extreme position?

**Archbishop:** Would that all of us who receive ecclesiastical revenues held to this same extreme! It would be far better than leaving inheritances built on the wealth of the poor.

**Antronio:** Without a doubt, you have utterly dismantled my way of thinking and remade me anew. Since that is the case, I beg you to tell me how I ought to spend my income properly.

**Archbishop:** Read the Sacred Scriptures, where God declares His will regarding this matter in many places, and act according to what you read.

**Antronio:** What do you mean by Sacred Scripture?

**Archbishop:** The Bible, both the Old and New Testaments. In them, God commands us to use what He gives us to help those in need, and I see no mention of any other purpose. Since He makes no mention of anything else, we must believe that this is what He wills and what pleases Him. If we all focused solely on this, I assure you, we would strive to leave our memories in heaven, not on earth.

**Eusebius:** We have spent much time on this matter. Let us set it aside now, my lord, and tell me: what difference do you make between the commandments of God and those of the Church, regarding how they should be observed?

**Archbishop:** I will tell you. We are obligated to observe God's commandments both outwardly and inwardly, and with a willing and ready heart—so much so that, at the very least, we should delight in them in our spirits and find them sweet and pleasing, as they truly are.

As for the commandments of the Church, Juan Gerson teaches that it is sufficient to observe them outwardly. Even if one keeps them unwillingly, as long as he does so, he fulfills his duty to the Church, for she judges only external actions. Thus, a person does not sin if he says, "I regret that the Church commands me to fast today, for I would rather eat meat." Similarly, for other Church commandments, though he may dislike observing them, if he does so nonetheless, he fulfills his duty externally.

However, a person does sin gravely if he says, "I regret that God commands me to love my neighbor as myself, for I would rather love myself more," or "I regret that God forbids stealing, for I would rather steal." The same applies to the rest of the divine commandments.

**Antronio:** So, by this reasoning, if I see someone eating meat during Lent because of illness and I wish I could do the same, do I sin?

**Archbishop:** That depends on the intent behind your desire.

**Antronio:** What if I desire it only for the sake of my health, since fish is harmful to me?

**Archbishop:** Then you do not sin, because your desire is simply that the Church had not made that commandment, as it is detrimental to your bodily health—and perhaps even to your spiritual well-being. But despite that, you still obey the Church's command.

**Eusebius:** As for the commandment of fasting, I admit you are right. But regarding the obligation of confession, I know that it is of no benefit to someone who confesses unwillingly.

**Archbishop:** That is true—it does no good even for the one who confesses merely to comply with the Church. What I have been explaining concerns only the outward fulfillment of the commandments. One who confesses unwillingly will not be punished by the Church, but God will certainly punish the one who refrains from stealing only out of reluctance, rather than out of love for His command.

**Antronio:** And what about someone who unwillingly goes to Mass on a feast day? Do you think he fulfills his duty?

**Archbishop:** Before the Church, he certainly does. And in some cases, he may even fulfill his duty before God. Consider a person who is engaged in some holy and good work, where he sincerely believes he is greatly serving God. If he is reluctant to leave that work in order to fulfill the Church's command to attend Mass, he still fulfills his obligation to both the Church and to God.

Father, if you can give me a heart that is right and discerning, one that directs all its actions solely toward God—as all Christians should—then I assure you that all of these matters will fall into place.

**Antronio:** I believe you, as you explain it. But tell me—do you apply this same reasoning to the payment of tithes?

**Archbishop:** You already know my position on that.

**Antronio:** No, truly, I do not.

**Archbishop:** Then if you do not know, it is a great impiety to excommunicate your parishioners over tithes while not believing that they fulfill their obligation, even if they pay them unwillingly.

**Antronio:** I must say, even if for no other reason, I would believe everything else you have said about the observance of the Church's commandments—because in all of it, you speak with great reason. But tell me, would you be pleased if all these things were taught openly to the people so that they might learn to observe each commandment rightly?

I truly believe you would not be more pleased with anything else.

**Archbishop:** Certainly, nothing would please me more.

**Antronio:** I believe that. But now, tell me—what devotions do you think should be taught to Christian children as soon as they begin to understand and recognize things?

**Archbishop:** First of all, you should teach them to devote themselves to loving God above all things and their neighbor as themselves. They should be drawn to and fall in love with God's law, resolve within themselves to do good to all as much as they are able, and never to harm anyone.

**Antronio:** But that is not devotion—it is a commandment of God.

**Archbishop:** That is true—it is indeed a commandment of God. But what I mean is that just as some people place their devotion in unnecessary fasts and practices that God has not commanded, so too should you teach children to place their devotion in what God has commanded—so deeply that they observe these precepts not as mere duties but as voluntary acts, delighting in them and fulfilling them with full affection and love.

**Antronio:** That is well said. But I was not asking about that kind of devotion, but rather about the kind commonly practiced.

**Archbishop:** That is precisely why I speak of this devotion. For one who does not have this kind of devotion will find little benefit in the other—but one who possesses this devotion has no need for anyone to tell him which other devotions he ought to adopt.

Believe me, Father, the most important foundation you should instill in children's hearts is love for what is good and hatred for what is evil. Then, you should firmly impress upon them the law of God in such a way that it can never be uprooted from their hearts.

As for other devotions—prayers, fasts, and similar practices, which are all secondary and voluntary, without obligation—you should allow each person to choose according to what most pleases them. But even with these, you must always ensure that the prayers of those you instruct are wise and discerning and that they ask God only for what serves His glory and their own salvation. They should not always repeat their prayers with the same words, but rather, they should pray with the words that their heart, guided by its needs, teaches them.

For you must understand that the fervent desire of the soul reaches the ears of God, not the noise or abundance of words.

**Antronio:** Then, according to this, you would not want people to use prayer books or prayer beads unless they are obligated to?

**Archbishop:** I am not saying that at all. Let those who wish to use them do so freely. But to tell you the truth, I would not consider it wrong for someone not to pray from a book or with beads—if I saw that they lived righteously. Nor would I consider it good if someone prayed frequently in either way yet had nothing else to show as a sign of being a true Christian.

I say this because I know many who, if you see them in church with their prayer books and beads, you would think they were Saint Jeromes. Yet as soon as they leave—or even while still in the church, right after finishing their Our Fathers and Psalms—they have such loose tongues in gossiping about their neighbors, in speaking lies, wickedness, and foolishness, that it is truly lamentable.

**Eusebius:** That must be because they have trained their tongues to rush through Psalms, and now they cannot restrain them when speaking of other things.

**Archbishop:** Whatever the reason, in the end, they will find themselves deceived, no matter how diligently they pretend, unless they abandon their wicked habits. I take comfort in knowing that there is an eternal life of joy for the righteous and an endless death of sorrow for the wicked.

**Antronio:** Even with all that you say, I am sure you would still approve that all Christians pray the Our Father and that it be explained to them thoroughly.

**Archbishop:** Indeed, not only do I approve of it—I hold it to be an absolute necessity. But only after they have learned what I have already mentioned, which is more fundamental and more necessary for them to know.

For in order for their prayer to be pleasing to God, they must first go through everything we have discussed. Then, once they are rightly prepared, it is most fitting that they learn to pray. Likewise, it is right that they understand what they are praying, and for that reason, the Our Father must be explained to them briefly, so that they may both pray it and comprehend it.

**Antronio:** On that point, I fully agree with you. But now, tell us—how do you think this brief explanation of the Our Father should be given?

**Archbishop:** I will explain it as God grants me understanding. May it please Him that my words are fitting, so that both you and I may be satisfied and content.

**Antronio:** There is no doubt that we will be pleased and satisfied with whatever you say.

**Archbishop:** Then, with that confidence, I say that it is right for all to know and understand the Our Father in this manner:

First of all, every Christian must know that this prayer was composed by our Redeemer, Jesus Christ Himself. This happened when His disciples approached Him and asked Him to teach them how to pray. Then, after instructing them not to multiply words in their prayers, He taught them this prayer. For this reason, the Our Father must be esteemed above all other written prayers combined.

In this prayer, Jesus Christ, our Lord, teaches us how we ought to pray. The nature of Christian prayer should be concise in words but rich in meaning—such is the true prayer of a Christian.

We are also shown what we ought to pray for, namely, that the entire prayer consists of nothing other than what pertains to the glory of God and the salvation of our souls and those of our neighbours.

Having said this, it is fitting to explain what every Christian ought to consider when reciting this prayer; and thus, with this consideration, it shall be set forth in the manner in which you ought to teach it, for I have ordered that it be taught in this way. You must know that this entire prayer is divided into seven petitions, which we shall indicate as we proceed. Therefore, when the Christian says:

"Father"—after having considered the supreme goodness of God, who delights in being called Father by His enemies, who daily offend Him in His presence—he must consider whether his deeds are those of a true son; and if he does not find them to be so, let him be confounded and humbled before God, and let him acknowledge his lowliness and misery.

When he says "our," let him remember that by this word he shows that all who call upon this same name, and are able to do so, are his brothers; and then let him carefully examine whether he treats them all as brothers, and whether he loves them as such from a sincere heart. When he finds himself lacking in this, let him, with living tears—not only of the eyes but of the heart—ask God to give him a spirit of love with which to love his brothers.

When he says: "who art in heaven," let him remember the exile in which he finds himself, and let him truly long to go to that heavenly homeland, to enjoy the delightful vision of the Eternal and Sovereign God, where joy and rest are perfect and complete, for there one rejoices without fear of loss; of which joy, even here in this world, God gives the soul certain fore-tastes so that, being enamoured with their sweetness, it may despise all the things of this world and regard its pleasures and delights as false and vain.

When he comes to say: "Hallowed be Thy name," let him consider that what he here asks of God is that He not permit him or anyone else to think, say, do, hold, or propose anything except that which is directed to the glory of God; and that in all things, by His grace, he may act with regard to His love and fear, for in this way the name of God is hallowed—when we become holy.

This is the first petition, and I am expressing it as briefly as I can, for in order that all may better retain it in memory, it is necessary that it be declared to the people often and in few words—especially to children.

**Eusebius:** It seems to me the best approach in the world that you are taking; and since it is so, proceed, sir, with your explanation.

**Archbishop:** I am willing; but it is necessary that you pay close attention. For since the name of God cannot be hallowed unless the Spirit dwells and reigns in our souls, therefore the second petition follows immediately, in which we pray thus: "Thy kingdom come." Here every Christian must understand that what he asks with these words is that God would deliver all men from the most cruel tyranny exercised over them by the devil, the world, and the flesh, by which they are led wherever those forces will, and even, at times, as if dragged by the hair; and likewise that God would will for His Spirit to reign and be the absolute Lord over all of us.

It is also necessary for them to know that this kingdom of God in our souls is nothing other than a voluntary subjection and complete obedience to God Himself, and a true peace, a marvellous rest, and a perfect satisfaction. Let them also understand that the reason they ask this of God is so that, with the tyranny of the devil broken and sin cast far away, their soul might remain free and pleasing before His Majesty, and thus become a living temple of God, where no one reigns but God alone—in such a way that, through both outward and inward obedience, it becomes a kingdom in which God reigns. This is a most profound truth: that if we were able to grasp how great and how precious is the good the soul possesses when it has God as its King and Lord, we would utter these words with such burning desire and such fervent zeal that our very entrails would be torn and our hearts broken in longing for their fulfillment. For the love of God alone, I entrust this to you, parish priest, that you earnestly exhort all to pay careful attention to this matter, for their life—and much more than life—is at stake in it.

And so, because God does not reign in our souls except when they are fully obedient to Him, both inwardly and outwardly, and because to attain this kingdom it is necessary to do the will of God, Christ Jesus, our God and Lord, taught us to say in the third petition: "Thy will be done on earth as it is in heaven."

Here the Christian must consider that, because by his very nature he is inclined to evil and to disobedience against God—and is grieved when God corrects and chastises him—he therefore asks God to grant him His grace, so that he may willingly consent to the fulfillment of God's will in him, as if saying: "Eternal Father, even though my sensitive flesh resists, heed it not—do what You will. Give me whatever discipline You desire—fulfill Your will and not mine! I do not wish mine to be done in any way, for it is always contrary to Yours, which alone is good, just as You alone are good, and mine is always evil, even when it seems to me to be very good."

**Eusebius:** I know that this is not the only area in which we ought to desire that the will of God be fulfilled.

**Archbishop:** That is true; but I told you this first because it is in matters like this that we find it most difficult to submit to the will of God. And whoever obeys God in this will more easily obey Him in everything else.

Thus, the Christian here asks that God's will be done in all things, absolutely—on earth as it is in heaven, where all are obedient to God. And they do this with joy and wholehearted willingness, because their will is fully conformed to God's. So I assure you that whoever sincerely prays these words and truly desires their fulfillment, as I have described to you, is not doing a small thing.

**Antronio:** As for me, I believe I truly pray them sincerely.

**Archbishop:** I believe that too, but I'm not so sure that you feel them as sincerely as you say you pray them.

Now then, returning to our subject: because for man to have such complete and firm conformity with the will of God is something beyond human strength, our Lord advised us to say the fourth petition in this way: "Give us this day our daily bread."

When the Christian speaks these words, he should understand that what he is asking for is grace to fulfill God's will—for this is the spiritual bread that sustains and gives life to our souls. This bread is the grace of the Holy Spirit, without which our souls cannot be pleasing to God even for a single moment. The soul is wonderfully sustained by it. And when, through this bread, our souls bear the image of Jesus Christ—who is the true and heavenly bread—they will be able, joyfully and completely, to break and subdue their own wills. They will also find any persecution that God sends them to be sweet and bearable.

Ultimately, the Christian should ask God in this petition to send true and holy teachers who will distribute to the Christian people the bread of sound Gospel doctrine—pure and clear, not corrupted or defiled by human opinions and passions. And as you can see, the need for this is indeed very great.

**Eusebius:** So great, in fact, that it could not be greater. And since you say it so well, I won't interrupt you. Please go on, for I am greatly pleased with the way you are explaining everything.

**Archbishop:** Because this heavenly bread should not be given, nor can it be given, to dogs—that is, to those who are defiled with sin—the fifth petition admonishes us to say: "Forgive us our debts, as we also forgive our debtors." In this, every Christian must take great care; for what he asks here must come from a full awareness of his sins and faults, which he asks God to forgive. Once cleansed from them, he may sit at the table of the children of God and partake of this heavenly bread, which is only for those whom God has forgiven and accepted as His own.

And because, without this command, our souls cannot freely walk through the trials of this world—and this command is given only to those whom God accepts as His own, and He accepts only those whom He forgives—and because, no matter how holy we may be, we always have something to be forgiven, it is necessary that we ask Him daily to forgive us. And in asking, we must also acknowledge that we indeed have something that needs forgiving.

And another thing must be understood here: we are not worthy of God's forgiveness simply because we forgive our debtors—that is, those who offend us. Rather, it is because God, in His infinite goodness and mercy, has willed to forgive us under this condition, that is why we are forgiven. So, it is necessary for us to forgive our neighbors if we wish to be forgiven by God, but we must never think that it is because we forgive that God forgives us. To believe that would be to attribute to ourselves what belongs to God alone.

I know some people—who think themselves very holy and wise—who, when they are at odds with someone and unwilling to forgive, say that they simply skip this part of the *Pater Noster*. Have you ever heard anything more foolish or senseless in your life? They have no fear of calling God "Father" while being children of Satan. They want and ask for the heavenly bread—which is given only to the pure in heart—but they are afraid to ask God to forgive them, lest He hold them to the condition they are unwilling to meet.

**Antronio:** By my life, I used to do just that every time I was at odds with one of my companions! And I never thought I was doing anything wrong.

**Archbishop:** Well, make sure you never do it again.

**Antronio:** I agree. But tell me, do you think it's better to skip the whole *Pater Noster*, or just that part?

**Archbishop:** Yes, better to leave out the entire prayer than to fall into that new superstition. Unless you're willing to put away your anger toward your brother, you should not pray this at all—except that you must not stop asking God for the grace to overcome yourself and to let go of that anger. Still, it would be far better if you simply forgave him and let go of the resentment; then you could pray the whole prayer rightly.

**Antronio:** But what if it's not in my power? What if I simply can't let it go?

**Archbishop:** If it grieves you that you cannot yet let go of the resentment you hold against him, then yes, you may say the whole prayer—and ask God to help your good will. Since He has given you the grace to desire what is good, ask that He give you grace to carry it out.

**Antronio:** Truly, I swear you've given me new life by saying that. I'll make use of this for myself and for others.

**Archbishop:** May God will it so. Now pay close attention, and we'll continue.

Since we have already asked God to forgive us, we must remember that *perseverance* in doing good is what is crowned in the end. But this perseverance is not something we can produce from ourselves, for by nature we are inconstant, weak in faith and trust, and quick to fall into temptation. That is why the sixth petition teaches us to say: "Lead us not into temptation."

**Archbishop:** When the Christian says these words, it is necessary—if he wishes them to have the effect for which they are spoken—that he first recognize the great weakness of his own strength, as well as the immense power and variety of temptations that come from the devil, the world, and the flesh. With this understanding, he should realize that what he is asking of God in this petition is to be upheld and preserved by His hand, and that He not allow him ever to be overcome by any temptation or dragged down into sin. Rather, that God grant him the grace of perseverance, so that he may fight manfully until death.

Now, since we know that God is just, and that He must therefore punish us for our sins—and that we must endure that punishment—it follows that our sin, which dwells in our members, is the cause of such chastisement.

For this reason, the final petition immediately follows, teaching us to say: "Deliver us from evil."

Here, the Christian, with the awareness I have just described, must give special attention and understand that what he is asking of God is this: since the evil that dwells in our flesh is what causes us to be tempted, to fall into temptation, and to be punished because of it, he asks that God, by His supreme power, would deliver him from this evil. That, being set free from all evil and sin, he may be, together with the lovers of Jesus Christ, a sanctifier of God's name; that he may also be the kingdom of God; that he may fulfill God's will in all things; that he may eat and be sustained by the daily bread of the grace of the Holy Spirit; that sin may never dwell in him without being immediately forgiven; and that he may not be overcome by temptations, which we cannot be entirely free from while we live in this world.

**Eusebius:** That seems to me a very new way of explaining it.

**Archbishop:** It's not as new as you might think, and in my view, it is better than any I have read, and more fitting.

**Eusebius:** Why do you think so?

**Archbishop:** I'll tell you. And so you can better judge it, I'll first share two other common interpretations. One is that this means "deliver us from all evil"; and here theologians make their distinctions, saying that it refers not to the evil of punishment but to the evil of guilt. I won't delve into that. But according to those who know Greek—the language in which the evangelists wrote—the distinction is beside the point. For this reason, Erasmus, in his translation of the New Testament, renders it as "deliver us from that evil one", meaning the devil. That's the second interpretation.

Both are, in my opinion, holy and good; but to my judgment, the one I've just given you is more fitting—because otherwise, it seems we are not asking for anything more in this petition than we did in the previous one.

**Eusebius:** How so?

**Archbishop:** He who asks God to deliver and keep him from falling into temptation—don't you think that he is also asking to be delivered from the devil?

**Eusebius:** Yes, without a doubt.

**Archbishop:** Then you would say the same of the other interpretation.

**Antronio:** Please, sir, for the love of your life, don't speak any further on this. I am perfectly satisfied with what you've explained. No need for more replies.

**Archbishop:** Very well, I will do as you say. To conclude, then, I say that it is most fitting that after we have asked God, in the previous petition, not to allow us to fall in temptation, we now ask Him in this one to deliver us from the evil that temptation brings—that is, the evil inclination that came to us through the sin of our first parents.

**Eusebius:** I assure you that although I did question your explanation, I've been thoroughly pleased with it.

**Archbishop:** Very good. Let our conclusion be this: that when we say "Amen", it is a word of confirmation—a complete affirmation and wholehearted request for all that has been said. And furthermore, if we wish to obtain the fruit of this prayer, we must recall that it was Jesus Christ Himself who taught us this manner of prayer. And that He also promised to grant what we ask, provided we ask rightly. And remembering this, we must hold firm hope that God, in order to fulfill His word, will grant us what we ask of Him through this prayer.

**Antronio:** Tell me, what if I cannot believe that God will hear me?

**Archbishop:** Do as the man did who brought his demon-possessed son to Jesus. When Jesus said to him, "If you can believe, all things are possible to him who believes," the man replied, "Lord, I believe—help my unbelief."

**Eusebius:** Truly, that was a fine reply—and you've explained the *Pater Noster* most excellently. I promise you, whoever reflects on these things each time they pray it will greatly build up their soul.

**Antronio:** That's certainly true. But how could someone fulfill the obligation of praying all the *Pater Nosters* and *Ave Marías* that are prescribed to us, both for those in holy orders and even for laypeople, if they had to reflect on all that each time? They wouldn't finish even one in an entire day! And what about lay-people who have the devotion of praying the rosary, and other such practices?

**Archbishop:** That question, you can see, is beside the point.

**Antronio:** Yes, I see that clearly—no doubt at all; and I only said that to see what you would say. But now I'm fully resolved to do whatever you tell me. And since I've decided to trust you in all things, I beg you to explain the *Ave María* and the *Salve Regina* in the same way that you explained the *Pater Noster*, because I am extremely devoted to Our Lady.

**Archbishop:** Those are things that need no further explanation, beyond understanding their Latin. So, for you, since you understand Latin, that's enough. For others, have them translated into the common tongue, and make sure they learn them in that form—that will suffice for them as well.

As for the devotion you say you have toward Our Lady, I hold that to be a very good thing; and in that, I wouldn't want you to outdo me. But I wouldn't want you to be like many I know, who pride themselves on being devoted to Our Lady, while at the same time living as her mortal enemies.

**Antronio:** What do you mean by that?

**Archbishop:** I'll explain. I know many people who are entangled in countless vices and who show no outward sign of being Christians, except for saying that they are devoted to Our Lady. And with the confidence they place in this so-called devotion, they believe they're free to commit whatever wickedness they please. That is why I often say that those who dishonor Our Lady the most are precisely those who have such devotions in this manner. Because those who truly revere her and are truly devoted to her strive, as much as they are able, to imitate her humility, her chastity, her charity, and her purity. That honors her far more than hearing many Masses in her name, reciting many prayers, or fasting many days—though all of that is good. But what foolishness it is for someone to be full of vice and still consider himself devoted to Our Lady just because he prays some prayers and fasts on certain days! Truly, that is a mockery and one of the greatest abominations in the world.

**Antronio:** If that is what you say, then I do not think you've read the book of miracles that Our Lady has performed for people who had exactly that kind of devotion you just criticized.

**Archbishop:** Yes, I've seen it, and I've read a good part of it. And when I think about how that little book gives foolish people an excuse to persist in their sins, I cannot help but say: bad luck to the one who wrote it, and to the first who printed it.

**Antronio:** Why would you say that?

**Archbishop:** Because something so contrary to the Gospel should never be allowed among Christians.

**Antronio:** And where do you find it to be contrary to the Gospel?

**Archbishop:** Let me explain. Saint Paul, among many other relevant teachings—some echoed by the evangelists—states plainly that neither the sexually immoral, nor the greedy, nor those entangled in sin will inherit the kingdom of God. Yet your little book recounts stories of individuals marked by all the very vices the Apostle condemns—some even worse—and claims that because one of them recited the *Ave Maria* daily, he was admitted into heaven at the hour of death. Could there be a more misleading notion of devotion?

**Antronio:** As God is my witness, you are entirely right; I had never considered it from that perspective.

**Archbishop:** Now tell me, in all honesty: if someone were to read that or something similar—of which many examples exist—and actually believe it, would he not conclude that simply reciting another *Ave Maria* permits him to live as immorally as he pleases?

**Antronio:** Indeed; and I might even be living proof of what you're describing.

**Archbishop:** Frankly, I do not understand how bishops and ecclesiastical leaders can remain at ease with their consciences while allowing such things to persist. And if they are aware of them, I do not understand why they have not taken steps to correct them.

**Eusebius:** Then why haven't you, since you are a bishop yourself, addressed the issue?

**Archbishop:** Until now, I have been occupied with other pressing matters and have not been able to address it directly. But give me the responsibility, and you shall see what I will do with that little book and others like it.

Now, setting that aside, know this, Father Curate: for devotion to be true and worthwhile, it must originate in God. The first and foremost effort of every person should be to seek this grace from God. Only then should he pursue additional devotions. Otherwise, mark my words: he will remain submerged in the sea of vice, lacking the oars of faith and the breath and light of charity to carry him safely to shore.

**Antronio:** In my case, it seems I went out seeking honor and came back shamed—and rightly so. I had hoped to gain some credit with you by presenting myself as devout, but the result has been quite the opposite. It is clear to me now that your devotion to God is so sincere that only that which is perfect and wholly grounded in Him can satisfy you.

**Archbishop:** Indeed, I do not see how anyone could be satisfied with any form of devotion unless it is genuinely and solely directed toward God.

**Antronio:** Very well, then. I am content with this. Now I would like you to tell me what you promised to explain to me at the beginning.

**Archbishop:** What was that?

**Antronio**: When you said that you wished all Christians would be given a brief summary of the Holy Scriptures, you also mentioned that you would explain how you envisioned it should be done.

**Archbishop**: You speak the truth; I did promise you that, and now I am prepared to fulfill my word.

**Antronio**: You speak in a manner consistent with who you are. So then, I first wish you would tell me the purpose for which you want this to be communicated to the people.

**Archbishop**: The purpose is that these sacred truths: being holy and good in themselves and leading us to the knowledge of God: might take root in the tender hearts of the young. Thus, their souls, grounded on such a foundation, would not easily fall from innocence. They would grow to love the law of God from what they heard spoken of it, and they would likewise grow to abhor the tyranny of the devil: as something evil, corrupt, and destructive.

Another benefit would be this: that by being engaged with these things, they would develop a taste for them. In doing so, through this practice, they would abandon the kinds of reading many now pursue: some books that lead them to become not Christian, but worldly, vain, and immoral; and others that foster a form of Christianity more ceremonial than genuine. At the very least, I promise to begin paying close attention to what books my parishioners are reading. For, as I said before, the disposition we form is shaped by the books we engage with.

**Antronio**: You speak well, and I trust you will do as you say. In the meantime, I beg you, my lord: tell us how you would present this summary of Holy Scripture. I would like you to express it in the same way you would wish it to be said to all.

**Archbishop**: I will gladly do as you ask. In my view, it would be fitting to present it in this way:

Since, by the goodness of God, my dear brothers, we are Christians, the primary and most consistent occupation of a Christian ought to be in the law of God, which is contained in the Holy Scriptures. For only Scripture reveals to us the will of God—and only Scripture, without the omission of a single letter, is written by the Holy Spirit. Of all the writings in the world, only this one we are bound to believe entirely, without exception.

Therefore, I will now tell you briefly what is contained in it, without going into detailed particulars: those you will read for yourselves when, by God's will, you are older.

So then, you must listen carefully, because what you are about to hear is entirely drawn from what was taught and dictated not by some wise man, but by the Holy Spirit Himself. These are not tales from the Indies or from Syria, but truths that have come from the heights of heaven.

And since this is so, be attentive and know this: we have one God, who is supremely good, and is goodness itself: supremely powerful, and is omnipotence itself: who, just as He never had a beginning, likewise will never have an end.

This God, in His eternal wisdom, created all things out of nothing: and this He did with ease, for His will is His power. Thus, in merely willing them to be, they came into existence. In this way He created the heavens and the earth and all that is in them: and He continually upholds all these things by His power, for they would perish if He did not sustain them.

He also created angelic spirits to stand before His majesty as His ministers. Among them was one of exceptional rank, whom we call Lucifer. This angel, driven by reckless and presumptuous pride, desired to set his throne alongside that of the Most High and to be like God. As punishment for his mad and rebellious ambition, God cast him and those other angels who joined in his wickedness out of heaven: assigning them to a place where they would suffer grievous torment and affliction forever.

After this, seeing that the thrones forfeited by the fallen angels remained empty, God willed to create mankind so that those who obeyed Him might inherit them. And because those seats had originally been lost through pride, He ordained that they should now be gained through humility. So, from a small portion of earth, He formed the first man and breathed into him the breath of life: He named him Adam, meaning "man." Then, causing Adam to fall into a deep sleep, God took one of his ribs and from it formed a woman, whom He named Eve.

These two were created in a state of innocence and placed in the earthly paradise—a wondrous and delightful garden. There God commanded them to eat freely from the fruit of any tree they wished—except for one tree in the middle of the garden, which was called the Tree of the Knowledge of Good and Evil. From that one, they were not to eat.

The evil angel, seeing that God had created these human beings to enjoy what he and his companions had lost, was moved by envy. He resolved to deceive them and lead them into disobedience, so that they would be punished by God just as he had been. Taking the form of a serpent, he used false and deceitful words to persuade Eve to eat the fruit of the tree that God had forbidden. After she ate, she gave some to her husband Adam, and he also ate. Because of this disobedience and their lack of faith—in believing the devil more than God—they lost their state of innocence and were cast out of the earthly paradise. And because of this, all of us who are born from them are conceived and born in sin: we become children of wrath and of the curse, subject to countless evil inclinations, labors, and sufferings—and ultimately, to eternal punishment.

Yet because our God is so merciful, even as He pronounced judgment, He also gave hope for a remedy. He told the devil that from the woman whom he had deceived would be born One who would crush his head and restore what the woman had lost. This was a prophecy concerning His only Son, Jesus Christ: our God and Lord.

After this, human wickedness began to spread—and so it happened that Cain, the son of Adam and Eve, out of envy murdered his brother Abel. As the human race multiplied, so did evil increase—until finally, after many years, God, angered by the sins of mankind, resolved to destroy the world with a flood. Finding only one righteous man in all the earth—whose name was Noah—God commanded him to build an ark so that he and his household might be saved. Noah obeyed. Then God sent such a great flood upon the earth that it lasted for forty days and forty nights without ceasing. The waters rose fifteen cubits above the highest mountain in the world, and so all was destroyed—only those who were in the ark that Noah had built according to God's command were saved—Noah and his wife, his three sons and their wives, along with the animals that God had instructed Noah to bring with him.

These descendants then began to multiply and fill the earth. Soon, however, there arose wicked giants who, driven by pride, attempted to build a great tower. In response, God destroyed their plan—He brought down the tower and scattered them across all parts of the world.

During this time, God called a just and holy man named Abraham out of his homeland and away from his relatives: He led him to the land of Palestine. To Abraham, God made great promises, all of which Abraham believed—and for this reason, his faith is highly praised in Holy Scripture.

Abraham had a son who was no less godly and beloved by God—he too was greatly blessed by the Lord. His name was Isaac. Isaac, in turn, had a son who was first called Jacob—but after wrestling with an angel, his name was changed to Israel. From him the Jewish people later took the name "Israelites."

Jacob had twelve sons, one of whom was named Joseph. Jacob loved Joseph more than any of his other sons, which stirred up envy among his brothers. They conspired against him and sold him to traders on their way to Egypt. But God granted Joseph such favor and success in Egypt that, within a few years, he rose to be the most powerful man in Pharaoh's court—second only to the king himself.

Then a severe famine struck the land where Jacob and his family lived. Jacob sent his sons to Egypt to buy grain: there they recognized their brother Joseph, the very one they had sold. Joseph showed them remarkable mercy and honor: he instructed them to return and bring their father and the entire household to Egypt, where he would provide abundantly for all their needs. They did so: Jacob and his entire family moved to Egypt, where Jacob later died. He left behind twelve sons, from whom the twelve tribes of Israel were named. One of them was called Judah: and from him the Jews took their name.

All these patriarchs were saved through faith in Jesus Christ, whom they expected would one day come to redeem them—just as we are saved through faith in the same Christ, who has already come.

While Joseph lived, the people of Israel were treated with great kindness and favor in the land of Egypt. But after Joseph died, and the king who had favored him also passed away, the new kings of Egypt began to oppress God's people. And the more the Israelites grew in number—by the strength God gave them—the more the Egyptians, as instruments of evil, afflicted them.

Then, moved by mercy, God took pity on the suffering of His people and sent them a holy and just man named Moses to lead them out of bondage. After God had afflicted the whole land of Egypt with terrible and devastating plagues—because Pharaoh had hardened his heart and refused to let the people go—He finally gave this command: the Israelites were to pretend they were celebrating a wedding, and each was to borrow many gold and silver jewels from their Egyptian neighbors. That night, without the Egyptians realizing, they secretly fled.[3]

Such was the immense love God had for this people—and the favor He showed them, even though they were sinful and disobedient—that He gave them a pillar of fire to light their way by night, and a cloud to shield them from the heat of the sun by day. He even parted the Red Sea so they could pass through on dry ground—and in that same sea, He drowned

---

3. **Editor's note:** There is no biblical warrant for this interpretation of the exodus from Egypt account, it may be possible this was drawn from some Talmudic or midrashic literature or it may be some inventive postulation by Roman Catholic exegetes.

Pharaoh and all the Egyptians who pursued them.

All these wonders God performed through the hands of Moses and his brother Aaron: one served as leader, the other as high priest. Yet despite all this, the Israelite people—being wicked and ungrateful—continually blasphemed and murmured against God as they journeyed through the wilderness toward the land He had promised them, which was Palestine. When they lacked water, He miraculously provided it; when they lacked food, He sent them quail from heaven and a most delightful manna—more excellent than any dish in the world.

But seeing that even with all these blessings He could not draw their hearts to love Him—since they continually turned again to idolatry—He resolved to give them a law filled with ceremonies, so they would be kept busy with these observances. Not that He, being Spirit, took pleasure in tabernacles and altars or in the multitude of sacrifices: but He gave the law to occupy them until the time was fulfilled in which He, in His eternal wisdom, had determined to send His own Son into the world as man: just as He had promised many times before.

God also gave them, on Mount Sinai, the Ten Commandments that we still keep today, along with many other precepts too numerous to mention. While they journeyed through these lands, God granted them great victories over their enemies. And before they entered the land He had promised them, after the death of Moses, He appointed Joshua as their leader. Through Joshua too, God worked great wonders. Under his leadership, the people of Israel crossed the Jordan River on dry ground with the Ark of the Covenant, and he led them into the land they had long sought. Time and again, because of the intercession of these leaders, God did not destroy that disobedient and rebellious people, although they continually provoked

Him with their persistent evil.

After Joshua's death, the people were governed by judges for a period of five hundred and fifty-five years. During this time, they experienced constant warfare: whenever they obeyed God's commands, they were victorious; but whenever they turned away from His will, they were miserably defeated.

During this period, God regularly sent them prophets and holy men to guide them in His law, but they refused to listen. Believing they would fare better, they asked God to give them a king. So He gave them Saul, who oppressed and mistreated them throughout his reign. Afterward, God gave them David as king—a most holy man—though even in his time they suffered continual war.

David was succeeded by his son Solomon, under whose rule the people enjoyed peace and prosperity. But after Solomon's death, the kingdom was divided, and because of their rebellion and wickedness, both kingdoms continually experienced hardship and affliction. They turned again to idolatry, and though God sent them holy prophets to guide them in the right path, they mistreated and even killed these prophets.

After many years and many kings, God permitted Nebuchadnezzar, king of Babylon, to capture His people and carry them away into exile, after destroying the great city of Jerusalem and the magnificent and costly temple that King Solomon had built. They remained in captivity for some time until God, in His mercy, delivered them and returned them to their land of Palestine. Gradually, they began to rebuild the city and the temple.

Finally, when the time was fulfilled—according to the promise that God had made both to this people in particular and to all mankind in general—to deliver them from the bondage and dominion of the devil and from the tyranny that led them into disobedience, God chose a most holy virgin from the tribe of Judah and the line of David, whose name was Mary. He sent His only begotten Son, so that through the work of the Holy Spirit, He might take on human flesh from her and become man. In doing so, He would make satisfaction to God for the offense committed by the first man, Adam, and restore for all of us the grace that we had lost through him. And by opening the gates of heaven—into which no man had previously entered—from then on, all who draw near to Him in faith and love would enjoy eternal blessedness.

The Son of God, then, was conceived by the power of the Holy Spirit, the angel Gabriel serving as the messenger. He willed to be born of a woman—though a virgin, and most holy—but poor and of lowly status by the world's standards. He chose to live in poverty and humility to teach us that we must gain grace through meekness and humility if we are to please God in this life; and by grace, attain glory—that is, to enjoy forever His delightful presence in eternal life.

This, then, is what I believe ought to be taught to every Christian. And though I have said it as briefly as I could, I fear I have been somewhat lengthy. To avoid being even more so, I have passed over the mysteries of the New Testament with only the briefest mention, though they too ought to be explained in much greater detail.

**Antronio**: Truly, I found all of it exceedingly good, and I was greatly delighted to hear you. Although I already knew most of what you said from hearing it in sermons, I had never understood it with such clarity or such a well-ordered connection from one part to the next. Blessed be God, who has endowed your soul with such high and noble wisdom.

**Eusebius**: Now tell us again: for what other purpose would you want this to be taught to all Christians?

**Archbishop**: So that, when people see all that God has done for mankind, and the patience with which He has endured and still endures them for so long, they may be stirred to love Him more and more. And also, so that by seeing the mercies and blessings He granted to the people of Israel—despite their constant rebellion—they may learn to place full trust in Him, believing that He, too, will show them favor and preserve them, if they wholly and sincerely give themselves to Him and place their confidence in His hands.

**Eusebius**: I had a feeling that earlier you had forgotten to mention this point, and that is why I asked you.

**Antronio**: As for me, all of this seems so new that I have not felt anything was missing. By the office I hold, I say this truly: you alone would be enough to convert half the world with your wisdom, insight, and holiness. I promise to repeat everything you have said to my parishioners just as you have said it—because, knowing the kind of man you are, I am sure you will not object to me asking you to have it all written down exactly as you have spoken it.

**Archbishop**: On the contrary, I would be more than pleased. For if I am anything, or if I have any worth, I would much rather use it for the benefit of others than for myself—since I know that is why God gave it to me, and that this is His will.

**Antronio**: You have said nothing that is not excellent. And since everything you have said has fit my purpose, I now ask you: how long has it been since you began learning and living out this doctrine you have taught us here?

**Archbishop**: Since I first had the judgment to discern between good and evil.

**Antronio**: And who was the one who first instructed you? I can hardly believe it was anything short of miraculous that God has taught you, since there are many theologians and learned men who would not know how to speak as purely and aptly as you have.

**Archbishop**: I am glad you asked me that, for I wanted you to know. You should know that my father had this custom: each morning, upon waking, he would gather his children—and even some others from the household—into a room, and there he would teach us, with great care, nearly all of the things I have told you today. After teaching them, he would question us about them, in much the same way you have questioned me. He used to say that just as a bishop is obliged to teach the Christians in his diocese, and a pastor the members of his church, so too he as father was obliged to instruct his children and household—especially since he was a learned man, and had not studied simply to make a living, but to edify his own soul and those under his care.

**Antronio**: May God bless such a man with a good life! Would to God that all bishops and pastors would reflect on this and engage in so holy a practice!

**Archbishop**: Well, now you see how I listened to these things day after day, and also repeated them to my brothers. And since I found them good and learned them—not only to know them, but to live them—they remained in my memory, just as you see. Besides this, my father had a teacher in the house to instruct me and my brothers in reading and writing. He, too, was a lover of all that was good and Christian. And through continual conversation and interaction with him, I see now that I gained much—indeed, I learned many of the things I have shared with you here.

**Eusebius**: Indeed, I have developed a great admiration for your father. May God reward him for it—I truly believe He already has. I wish there were many more like him. I have never in my life heard anything better. A man like that deserves to be held in the highest honour. I tell you, you owe far more to your father than if he had left you a fortune.

**Archbishop**: That I know very well. Blessed be God for it— especially when I see other fathers who make no effort to raise their children to be virtuous, thinking they have done enough by leaving them material wealth. I have never seen a greater cruelty—or rather, a greater impiety.

**Eusebius**: Truly, I know a man who puts all his energy and vigilance into securing a large inheritance for his son, yet refuses to spend even a pittance on a teacher to instruct his son in virtue and teach him how to live rightly. I do not know what kind of demonic blindness this is. Even if it were only so the son would know how to use that wealth properly, he ought to be taught to be a good man. How much more, then, considering that these men call themselves Christians, should they seek to be godly themselves—and ensure that their children are as well. And do not think this is just a rare case—if you look around, you'll find this is a common failing among almost all the wealthy.

**Archbishop**: Let me tell you something, and you will see that I owe even more to my father than you think. When he saw, as a boy, that I had a natural inclination for all that was holy and good, he worked diligently to ensure that this desire would grow rather than diminish. So he arranged for me to live in the household of that blessed archbishop I mentioned earlier— who, as you know, was deeply devoted to instructing children in godliness, as you can see from some of the writings he left behind.

**Antronio**: Yes, that's true—I have seen them.

**Archbishop**: Through my constant contact with that holy man, and by observing his conduct and piety, I made great progress in the things my father and my teacher had taught me. And if we had more time right now, nothing would please me more than to share with you some of the remarkable things about that blessed archbishop. They were so notable that any-one in this archdiocese could tell you about them if you asked.

**Eusebius**: Blessed are you, my lord, to have had such a father; and blessed is the man who had a son so willing to benefit from what his father taught him. Truly, if there were more people like your father in the world, we would need to go off to the Indies ourselves—for if they were doing what we are supposed to do, they would have no need to give us their estates. And if there were more teachers like the one you had, children would not fall into corruption so early, as they do now for lack of faithful instructors. And if we had more church leaders like the one you named, who earnestly sought the welfare of their people and households, there would certainly be more honesty, virtue, and true Christian character than we see today. But because of our sins, wicked fathers have no concern that their children become good; corrupt teachers can only pass on their vices; and from ambitious and greedy bishops, their people learn nothing but ambition and greed. This is a very certain and true rule.

**Antronio**: Everything you have said is entirely true. I only wish you would have added a word against the parish priests too— then I would have taken my share of the rebuke. But I suppose you left that out because, no matter how mild the reproach, given what we are, it would have been checkmate for us.

**Eusebius**: Well said! But now you must remain silent for a while so the Archbishop may tell us—this time for my benefit—how he conducts himself in his spiritual meditations.

**Archbishop**: In the same way that the prophet David did, and as Saint Paul instructs us to do.

**Eusebius**: Please explain that more clearly.

**Archbishop**: Read the Psalm of David that begins, *Blessed are the undefiled in the way* (Psalm 119), and you will see how the entire meditation and exercise of that most holy prophet consisted in reflecting on the commandments and the law of God. And you will find the same emphasis in many other psalms. If you read the epistles of Saint Paul, you will find that they also present no other form of contemplation. So you may be sure that this is true contemplation: for from this, the soul comes to know the supreme goodness, greatness, and mercy of God; from this, it also comes to understand its own frailty and misery. Here the soul learns what it owes to God, to its neighbor, and to itself. In short, there is no true good that cannot be reached through this continual contemplation. As for those other "imaginations"—of whatever kind—that some call contemplation, I do not know what they are or what fruit they bear, except a dry satisfaction that they have spent their time well. And I call it dry because from such exercises, the soul—who is supposed to benefit—comes away cold and barren.

**Eusebius**: And what book taught you this?

**Archbishop**: Experience.

**Eusebius**: Then, by that, I take it you have practiced such contemplations yourself.

**Archbishop**: Yes, indeed I have—and I do not regret it.

**Eusebius**: But if you do not believe them to be good, why do you not regret having practiced them?

**Archbishop**: For certain reasons, which I will one day share with you privately when we have the opportunity.

**Eusebius**: As you wish.

**Antronio**: I do not quite know what to say. I find you, sir, to be the complete opposite of every man I have ever spoken with in my life.

**Archbishop**: As long as you do not find me opposed to the doctrine of Jesus Christ, or to that of His Apostles or the Catholic Church, I care little for the rest. Besides, you will find many others who would say the same as I have.

**Eusebius**: I do not know what to say, except that you have also taught me how to contemplate. For I must tell you the truth: though I used to consider those imaginative practices you criticized to be good, your words have so persuaded me— as I reflect on them more and more—I find them so true that I cannot argue against them.

**Antronio**: You know, sir, it seems to me that every word you say is entirely fitting. And since that's the case, I beg you, tell us—by your life—what books in the vernacular you think I should recommend to my parishioners for reading.

**Archbishop**: They should read the *Book of Epistles and Gospels and Sermons for the Year*—though, to tell you the truth, I am not fully satisfied with the sermons, nor is the translation of the rest as it ought to be. They can also read the writings of the Carthusians, which contain much teaching from the holy doctors of the Church; and Erasmus' *Enchiridion*, as well as some of his shorter works available in the vernacular, such as the *Explanation of the Lord's Prayer*, a *Little Sermon on the Child Jesus*, and some of his *Colloquies*. Also, the *Contemptus Mundi*, attributed to Gerson; the *Letters of Saint Jerome*; the *Moralia* of Saint Gregory, which have recently been printed in the vernacular; and likewise, some shorter works by Saint Augustine.

**Antronio**: And would it not be suitable for them to read some of the devotional booklets and contemplative writings by other devout individuals?

**Archbishop**: I have no objection to them reading those. But I am not referring to such works right now—only to the books you should encourage your people to make familiar. And as I have already said—if you have followed my meaning—I am not a friend of the kind of imaginative spirituality those books often promote.

**Antronio**: Then I ask you to tell me how you yourself read the sacred books and the writings of the saints.

**Archbishop**: When I read one of the books you've mentioned, and I come across something that truly delights me, I reflect inwardly on the spiritual wealth I would possess if that virtue or truth were truly mine. Then, my spirit is immediately lifted in great and fervent desire to ask God to grant me that very grace which I find necessary for my soul. In this way, I turn my reading into prayer and contemplation. And I want you to know that, in my view, the person who makes a habit of reading and studying in this way will benefit more in one year than another might in a hundred. For this reason, whenever I pick up a book to study—especially if it is Sacred Scripture—I do so with deep reverence and humility, lowering my spirit before the presence of God. I earnestly pray that He would enlighten my understanding, so that whatever I comprehend may serve only for His glory, the edification of my soul, and the benefit of my neighbors. And truly, every time I do this, I close the book with a renewed desire for God and a fresh love for virtue.

**Eusebius**: I am greatly pleased to have heard this. With God's help, I will strive to imitate your method of study, and I will even encourage many others to do the same. And our parish priest will take care to follow my example as well.

**Antronio**: By my word, he had better. Though I have never been much inclined to study, I will be from this day forward.

**Archbishop**: Let's see now—why haven't you had an interest in study?

**Antronio**: I will tell you the truth. People say no one praises what he does not understand, and since I could grasp very little—or rather, nothing at all—from study, I simply could not take pleasure in it.

**Eusebius**: You have answered very well and to the point. But now you would do well to take up some form of study—not only for your own sake, but also for the benefit of your parishioners. Since they entrust you with their livelihoods, it is only right that you provide them with sound teaching. But you cannot teach them if you yourself are not well taught; and you cannot be well taught without effort and study.

**Archbishop**: He speaks absolute truth. Do not fail to follow this counsel.

**Antronio**: I agree. But tell me—how do you expect a man like me, who is past fifty, to begin studying grammar?

**Archbishop**: Wait—do you mean to say you don't know any Latin?

**Antronio**: I learned a little as a boy, but soon forgot it all.

**Archbishop**: Then how did you come to be ordained to celebrate Mass?

**Antronio**: I will explain. As a young man, I joined a religious order. I had a good voice, and when I reached the proper age, they had me ordained to say Mass—even though I did not know Latin, nor could I even read properly. As you know, friars are not examined by the bishop but by their own superiors. So I passed through with the others. Later, due to some disagreement—and also because I was not content there—I left the habit.

**Archbishop**: I assure you, that is a serious matter: that sacred orders would be conferred upon someone who cannot understand what he reads—even if he is a friar. As though friars had less need to know these things than others. At the very least, in my archdiocese, while I live, no one will be ordained—no matter who he is—unless I myself examine him, and examine him thoroughly. And not only will I examine what he knows, but before ordaining him, I will have a serious inquiry made into his life and conduct in the days leading up to the ordination. If I find that his life has been, and continues to be, in keeping with the Christian faith, and that he is also a man of learning and competence, then I will ordain him. But if he lacks any of these things—regardless of pressure from anyone—I will not even grant him minor orders.

**Eusebius**: May God grant you a good and long life—what you say is exactly what I long to hear! May it please God that you live many more years, so that you may reform this and many other matters where there is so much ruin—it is one of the greatest tragedies in the world. I truly believe there would be a very different kind of Christianity if all prelates acted as you do. But since no attention is paid to the things you have mentioned when it comes to those seeking ordination, they do nothing but turn out more clergy, and the people have come to treat it like a source of profit. As the number of clerics and friars increases, so does the disorder and corruption in their lives. Laypeople then take that as an excuse to live poorly themselves, and everything falls into decay. And to remedy it, there is no better solution than what you have just proposed. If the same standards were applied to the admission of friars, without doubt it would bring great benefit.

**Antronio**: All right then! Now answer me and leave church reform for another time.

**Archbishop**: As for you, I have only this to say: Since it's now too late for you to learn Latin, devote yourself diligently to books in the vernacular. And take into your company a person of sound learning and godly character, to whom you give half of your income, so that he may instruct you in what you ought to do. Do not take this the wrong way—I assure you, if you were one of my subjects, you would not get off so easily.

**Antronio**: Please do not say that, my lord—for I truly believe the greatest blessing I could have would be to be under your pastoral care, so great is the love I have come to bear for you. And since this is no doubt the case, I beg you to treat me not merely as one of your subjects, but as more than that, for I will count it a very great mercy. And what you have commanded me to do, I will do gladly—and even more gladly if the person you want me to take under my roof is chosen by your own hand.

**Archbishop**: I am very grateful for your good will—and truly, such goodwill obliges us to do much for you. As for the person you want me to provide, I will indeed give him to you—and such a one, I trust, that you will be most satisfied. What I strongly urge and charge you to do first is this: Determine in your heart to be a true and sincere Christian, in accordance with all we have discussed here. To do that, you will need to root out entirely those desires for worldly honour that still dwell in you—for such desires greatly hinder the soul that longs to soar toward heaven. You will do this easily if, just as those who serve the world turn their backs on God, you likewise turn your back on the world with firm resolve, thinking of nothing but how to serve and please God, paying no attention to anything the world or its admirers may say about you. For if you do this—if you become the kind of man God wants you to be—you will also strive to ensure that those placed under your care by God become the same. And in doing so, you will fully discharge your pastoral duty. To this end, place great trust in the man I will give you, for he is the kind of person who will know well how to instruct and guide you.

**Antronio**: My lord, with the grace of our Lord, I will strive to do everything you have commanded. And let me say—even as I speak—I am silently giving thanks to God for the mercy He has shown me, in bringing about this occasion for me to meet you, and for all the good and excellent things you have shared with me. I will serve Father Eusebio all my life, for he was the one who brought me to know you. Oh, blessed be the day you entered my church!

**Archbishop**: All right then! The friars are ringing for the close, and it would not be right to keep their doors open. If there is anything more to ask, do it now, for I have no more time to spare tonight, and tomorrow I will be far busier with certain matters regarding the college I am beginning to establish.

**Antronio**: Since that's the case—and so that I won't be left with any doubts—I ask you, my lord, to tell me whether, if I do everything you've commanded and advised, I may say Mass and receive the income from my benefice without scruple.

**Archbishop**: Yes, you may do both—what I have asked of you is not a change of vocation, but a change of conduct.

**Antronio**: Without a doubt, my lord, you have changed me so thoroughly that I suspect those who knew me before will not recognize me now. It pains me so much to part from you that I would gladly do nothing for the rest of my life but kiss your hands and feet. Blessed is the church that has gained such a bishop!

**Archbishop**: Very well. Go now in the peace of God. If you return another day, I will tell you other personal matters that will bring you joy.

**Antronio**: I will gladly do so—even if I lived much farther away. Since now is not the time for more, may God remain with your lordship.

**Archbishop**: May He go with you. And you, Father Eusebio, go with the parish priest and see that he is well received and shown great honour.

**Eusebius**: I will do as your lordship commands.

**Antronio**: Now that we're alone, I want to tell you something that has me utterly astonished. I simply cannot imagine what could have led the Archbishop to take on the charge of this church, being, as he is, such a good man—without greed, without ambition, and free of any vice—in short, a true Christian in every sense.

**Eusebius**: I will tell you the reason—and you will see it is more than sufficient. I assure you that, once you know it, you will value him even more for accepting the position than if he had refused it. You see, Father, those who are truly devoted to God must, in every way they can, strive to give themselves fully to His service, without regard to personal interest. And since nothing allows us to serve God more effectively in this world than to act as His stewards—both by winning new souls, rescuing them from the service of the devil, and by preserving those already gained—our highest aim should be precisely that. And to that end, we must choose the means that are most fitting. And since today there is no more effective means than becoming a bishop—with its authority and resources—a man does very well to accept such a position for that reason. Just as those who accept it for other purposes do very wrong. So, given that the Archbishop is the kind of man you have seen, don't you think it would have been wrong for him to refuse this dignity when it was offered to him (without his own seeking), especially when he is capable of doing so much good in the role?

**Antronio**: Without a doubt, you are entirely right in what you have said. I am deeply moved by your reasoning, and now I hold this good man in even higher esteem—seeing that he set aside his own comfort and peace in order to benefit others through toil and sacrifice. Truly, he owes much to God for having received such a noble spirit; and we owe much to him for placing himself so fully at our service.

**Eusebius**: I assure you, you are right to say so. And let me tell you: just as it is a very bad thing—and truly it is—for someone to seek out such dignities for their own glory and honour, so too I believe it is wrong when men who might do great good and serve God in such offices refuse them. For it seems that they prefer to live for themselves—caring only for their own ease—rather than for their neighbours and for God. Though, sadly, that happens all too rarely. And that is why people often think more highly of a good man who refuses these positions than one who accepts them—which, as it seems, was your error too.

**Antronio**: Yes, I was mistaken—no doubt about it. And now that I have been corrected in this, as in many other things, I would like to ask your advice on one more matter: what means can I use to distance myself from certain bad company I keep back in my town?

**Eusebius**: Look—we've arrived at the inn. Let's leave it here for now. We can speak further on that, and anything else you wish, later.

**Antronio**: So be it.

## THE END

# Juan de Valdés

Juan de Valdés (c. 1490–1541) was a Spanish religious writer and reformer closely tied to early Catholic renewal movements. Born in Cuenca, Castile, and often confused with his twin brother Alfonso, Juan emerged as a critic of ecclesiastical corruption through his early writings, such as *Diálogo de Mercurio y Carón* (c. 1528). Fearing the Spanish Inquisition, he fled to Naples in 1530 and later settled permanently, where his home became a vibrant center of literary and religious exchange. Although his friends encouraged him to pursue humanist fame, Valdés was more concerned with biblical interpretation and promoting a devout Christian life. Among his notable associates were prominent figures like Peter Martyr Vermigli, Marcantonio Flaminio, Vittoria Colonna, and Giulia Gonzaga. Valdés's influence extended to leading reformers such as Bernardino Ochino and Pietro Carnesecchi, shaping their views on justification by faith and spiritual renewal, even though he himself remained wary of aligning with the Lutheran schism.

Valdés' writings, including *Diálogo de la Lengua*, *Alfabeto Christiano*, and various biblical commentaries, placed him among Spain's foremost prose stylists. Though his works circulated mainly in manuscript during his lifetime, later Italian translations helped preserve his legacy despite Inquisitorial suppression. Accusations that he strayed from Catholic orthodoxy on doctrines like the Trinity arose only decades after his death, often based on ambiguous expressions or later interpretations, though scholars like Gaston Bonet-Maury note his explicit affirmations of orthodox beliefs. Valdés was ultimately less interested in speculative theology than in nurturing practical, personal piety, leaving a body of work that influenced generations of reform-minded Catholics and Protestants alike.

## ABOUT THE CÁNTARO INSTITUTE

*Inheriting, Informing, Inspiring*

The Cántaro Institute is a reformed evangelical organization committed to the advancement of the Christian worldview for the reformation and renewal of the church and culture.

We believe that as the Christian church returns to the fount of Scripture as her ultimate authority for all knowing and living, and wisely applies God's truth to every aspect of life, her missiological activity will result in not only the renewal of the human person but also the reformation of culture, an inevitable result when the true scope and nature of the gospel is made known and applied.